Talk and a course in oral work for GCSE

Theresa Sullivan
John Griffin
Paul Groves
Nigel Grimshaw

Longman

Contents

Assessment 1

To the teacher 1
To the pupil 8

1 Find out about people 10

How do we judge people? 11
Getting to know people 14
Interviews for magazines and television 15
Interviewing with a purpose 21
Interviews – a role-play 24
A consumer survey 30

2 Talking to people 34

Talking without hesitation 35
Talking with persuasion 36
Talks about hobbies, interests, jobs 37
Talks about politics, current affairs and issues 40
Telling a story 43
Giving precise instructions 49

3 Read it aloud 51

Your tone of voice 52
Clear speaking – reading with meaning 56
A formal reading 62
Reading a piece of information 63
The commentator's skill 67

4 Make a call 71

Using the telephone 72
Telephoning instructions 73
Buying by telephone 76
The telephone – coping with a problem 77
The telephone – making an arrangement 79

5 Have a good argument 81

What is a good argument? 82
Challenging an argument 84
Problem solving 88
Know your facts! 89
Points of view 90
A mock trial 92

6 A matter of tact 101

Choose your words carefully 102
Breaking bad news 106
Relationships 108
Suiting language to purpose 109
Speaking for different purposes 113

7 Working together – two role-plays 117

8 Finding out the truth 127

Asking questions 127
A role-play 128

Index 132

Assessment

To the teacher

Talk and Listen offers the widest variety of opportunities for developing oral and aural skills. This is the book's principal concern; and, we hope, will also be the teacher's. The compulsory oral component of GCSE offers new opportunities that have been denied to pupils in the past, particularly those taking GCE; but some of those opportunities could be lost if GCSE brings an atmosphere of continuous assessment into classrooms.

There are clear signs that the GCSE Examination Boards are as anxious as the teachers themselves about the difficulties of oral work assessment. The eventual decision to make Oral Communication a separately assessed subject, appearing as an endorsement on the certificate, is probably in itself a reflection of that anxiety.

This is intended as a general guide for assessment and is offered with the following caution:

If teachers are continually using checklists of objectives to assess pupils' work, there is a danger that assessment will be based on the number of the objectives achieved, rather than on the degree to which they have been satisfied. Often, the more categories by which a piece of work is judged, the less 'accurate' is the eventual mark. Teachers will need to take careful account of assessment objectives in the early stages (and this may initially involve constant reference to the Examination Boards' lists). However, there is no reason to suppose that an 'impression' mark – generally accepted as the most accurate method of assessment for continuous writing – should not become the best and safest method for oral work, provided that the work is of such variety that each aspect of oral work is given a principal role in some part of the course.

Talk and Listen contains four distinct kinds of oral activity:
1 Reading to an audience
2 Speaking to an audience

3   Role-play or simulation

4   Group discussion

The guiding principles and suggestions below are in no way pre-scriptive; they are based on our readings of all the GCSE Examination Boards' syllabuses.

Reading to an audience

Consider tone of voice, volume, clarity, pace and rhythm, eye-contact, gesture and timing; appropriateness to content and audience should be the principal criterion in each case. Audience response (not necessarily verbal) is obviously important, as is the degree to which the pupil has demonstrated a thorough understanding of what he or she is reading.

Each pupil should, at a minimum, have an opportunity to read to the whole group:

a   a passage chosen of his/her own work

b   a passage chosen by him/her from a work of literature

c   a passage of exposition/instruction/advice/argument/description, selected by the pupil from a folder of suitable pieces chosen by the teacher.

Speaking to an audience

Each pupil should be given the opportunity to relate, describe, report, evaluate and express opinion. The criteria outlined for 'Reading to an audience' should be applied, but content will assume greater importance.

Differentiation in English will be principally achieved by outcome; nevertheless, in assessing speaking to an audience, it should be recognised that certain tasks are inherently more difficult than others. The presentation of ideas with appropriate illustration is, for instance, more difficult than describing experience. This is implicitly acknow-ledged in Examination Boards' criteria. For instance:

Grade 5

... presenting facts and ideas in a recognisable order.

... describing experience in simple terms and stating what is felt and what is imagined.

Grade 1

... consciously ordering facts, ideas and opinions, and presenting them clearly and accurately for the benefit of a particular audience.

... describing and reflecting on experience and expressing effectively what is imagined.

Speaking to an audience offers clear opportunities for differentiation; and consideration of the degree of difficulty of the task could lead justifiably to a weighting in favour of the more difficult tasks in the assessment record.

Role-play or simulation

Interpersonal skills, such as the ability to listen sensitively, respond to other people's initiatives and recognise the particular context of a speech situation, are the bases for assessment. Since group work implies sensitive cooperation, both when listening and speaking, it is easier to assess the group rather than an individual's contribution.

It is probably unfair to attempt assessment of any more than three pupils' contribution to a large group at any one time. Sensitive listening can be shown by gesture as well as speech. Attempts to assess each individual's contribution to a large group may result in too great an emphasis being placed on an oral contribution and too little on reaction or non-verbal response.

Group discussion

Interpersonal skills again form the basis for assessment. The variety of tasks available, from a formal debate to an informal group chat, offers opportunities for assessing appropriate contact, tone and manner in a wide range of situations.

Diffident pupils often only show their ability in a situation where their opportunities to speak are built into the structure of the task. Therefore the more formal tasks, such as the debate or interview, should play at least as important a role in the overall assessment as the more informal ones.

Grade descriptions for oral work

These vary little between Examination Boards. The following is a compilation of several sets, with what may be regarded as the significant features. There are, of course, only five grades for Oral Communication.

Grade 5

The candidate has demonstrated *some ability* in
a conveying *simple* information
b presenting facts, ideas, opinions in an *orderly* sequence
c making comments of *some relevance* on what is heard, seen or read
d using *some variation* in speech style according to the situation
e recognising the *basic* difference between fact and opinion
f speaking audibly and intelligibly with *some sense* of *appropriate* intonation, tone and pace.

Grade 3

The candidate has demonstrated *competence* in
a understanding and conveying both straightforward and more *complex* information
b *consciously ordering* facts, ideas and opinions with clarity and accuracy
c *evaluating* spoken and written material and *highlighting* what is relevant for a *particular* purpose
d describing and *reflecting* upon experience and expressing *intelligibly* what is felt and what is imagined
e showing a good *understanding* of the significance and importance of *register*
f speaking audibly and intelligibly with a *marked sense* of appropriate tone, intonation and pace.

Grade 1

The candidate has demonstrated *expertise* in
a presenting simple, detailed and complex information in an *interesting*, *precise* and *authoritative* manner.
b presenting facts, ideas and opinions *logically*, *concisely* and *accurately* in a *variety* of situations and audiences
c *evaluating* what is heard, seen or read and *highlighting* and *reflecting* upon what is relevant for a *particular* purpose

d describing and *reflecting* upon experience, and communicating with *sensitivity* what is *imagined*

e *recognising* that words may signify more than they initially appear to say and *discerning the significance* of underlying assumptions and points of view

f showing *sensitivity to the audience* in communicating the language of others

g speaking audibly, intelligibly, lucidly and logically, with a marked sense of appropriate tone, intonation and pace.

Oral record cards

A record card for each pupil may be helpful and may be used as a checklist by the teacher. The model on pages 6–7 could be adapted to suit individual tastes and circumstances.

Note

The GCSE Examination Boards recognise that the final grade recommended to the external moderator will not necessarily reflect the mathematical total of the marks awarded for each activity.

This recognises implicitly the danger of an over-reliance on checklists and a mechanical adherence to the assessment objectives. It invites the use of an overall impression mark to weigh against the mark arrived at by subdividing each activity into categories.

Oral assessment record

Name:

Assessment category / Task description	Reading own work	Group discussion	Formal debate	Relating experience	Describing a process
Content	✓	✓✓			
Orderly presentation		✓			
Clarity	✓✓	✓✓✓			
Tone/pace	✗	?			
Appropriateness					
Non-verbal communication	✓	✓✓			
Audience/group response	✓✓	✓			

Interview in pairs	Group simulation	Presenting argument	Making a report	Unseen reading	Comment
					1 Certainly audible!
					2 Led group discussion – rather too dominant, but definitely in control!
	(The symbols are intended to help the teacher reach an appropriate mark for each piece. The marks are recorded on the assessment grid specified by each Examination Board.)				
					3 Showing more awareness of appropriate tone.
					(The comments should be positive, even when they imply omissions, such as 1.)

To the pupil

Self-assessment

The activities in this book are intended to help you enjoy the oral part of your course. Teachers can point out your strengths and weaknesses, but you can help yourself improve by checking your own performance after each activity.

Reading to the class

After a reading to the class, ask yourself these questions.

1 Did they hear me clearly?
2 Did I fully understand what I read?
3 Did I make them understand what I read?
4 Did I make it sound interesting?
5 Did I emphasise the important points?
6 Did I vary my tone of voice?
7 Did I look at the audience enough?
8 Did I emphasise my words with facial expressions and hand and body movements?
9 Were they interested in what I read?
10 Should I have chosen a different piece?

Speaking to a class

After speaking to the class, ask yourself these questions.

1 Had I prepared what I was going to say, in the right way? (Were any notes too sketchy, or too complicated to refer to?)
2 Should I have used more illustration – the blackboard or exhibits?
3 Did I read too much from my notes and not look at the class enough?
4 Did I develop my talk in a logical way?
5 Did I give enough examples to illustrate my points?
6 Did I feel confident or nervous? (Practice and good preparation will help overcome nerves.)
7 Did I speak too hurriedly or mumble?
8 Did the class hear me clearly?
9 Did they understand what I said? (Any questions they asked will help you to judge this.)
10 Did the class seem interested or bored by my talk?
11 Did I emphasise my words with facial expression?

Audience reaction is a good method of self-assessment. Discuss the various reactions of these soldiers. Do any of them seem interested? What can they be listening to?

Write ten lines of the talk they are hearing. Make it as boring or silly as you like.

Group discussion or role-play

After group activities, ask yourself these questions.

1 Did I listen carefully to what others were saying?
2 Did I watch and react to what they were doing?
3 Did what I say fit in with the way the group was working?
4 Did I act my part in the right way?
5 Did I say too little? (If you did, ask yourself whether this was because you were shy, other people said too much, or you felt unsure of what you should be doing.)
6 Did I say too much and prevent others having a fair chance?
7 Did the others listen and respond to what I said or did?
8 Did my opinions or my acting make a contribution to the group?

By asking yourself these questions you will be able to make clear to yourself the areas where you can improve. Remember that the amount you say is not as important as what you say and how you say it.

1 Find out about people

There are many reasons why we want to find out about people: to make friends, to be entertained, to test our opinions, to find out their suitability for a job. In this chapter you will be asked to:

- think about the way we make judgements on people
- take part in an exercise about getting to know people
- consider the techniques of interviewing for newspapers and television
- hold your own newspaper and television interview
- evaluate other groups' interviews
- consider the significance of body language
- decide what qualities are sought in a candidate for a job
- practise what you have learnt about job interviews
- evaluate job interviews presented by other groups
- take part in a role-play about choosing students for a teacher training course

How do we judge people?

When you first meet someone, how do you decide what sort of person he/she is?

1   *In pairs*, decide what importance you give to each of these when you are judging someone you have just met:

face as a whole	gestures
eyes	walk
hair	posture
ears	clothes
mouth	voice – tone/sound
height	accent
shape	behaviour/mannerisms
smile	

All these contribute to our first impressions of a person. Is it fair to judge on first impressions? What makes us change our first impressions? How important is what a person *says*? Or the way he/she says it?

2   The people in the following five photographs were given a part in a play which was thought to correspond with their appearance.

   In pairs, decide what kind of person each was being asked to portray.
   Is it reasonable to cast people like this for a play?
   Is it reasonable to make the same kind of judgements in real life?

Getting to know people

Interviewing

When interviewing people you may fail to find out what you want to know because you have not asked the right questions. One of the most important skills – particularly with someone who is not very communicative – is to think quickly and to find different ways of obtaining the information you think you are looking for. Try these warm-up exercises to test your own skill.

Warm up 1

STAGE 1   **The roles**

*Work in pairs and label yourselves **A** and **B**.*

A   You are a police officer. There has been a series of burglaries in the local shops. They may have all been done by the same person but you have no witnesses and no leads. Now, on a quiet Sunday afternoon, you receive news that there has been yet another burglary at a high street jeweller's and a witness is coming in to answer questions. Set up your office and decide what questions you are going to ask.

B   You are the witness. Read **A**'s instructions (above) and then your own instructions on page 33, while **A** is setting up the office. Do not tell **A** what you have read.

STAGE 2   Hold your interview. Stop the interview after fifteen minutes.

STAGE 3   **B** now tells **A** the facts if **A** has not already discovered them.

STAGE 4   Either in pairs or as a class, discuss what kind of questions are more likely to obtain the information. Who was the most successful at getting the information? Why? Is there anything to be learned from this exercise about interviewing techniques?

Warm up 2

Concentrate

*Work in pairs and label yourselves **A** and **B**.*

STAGE 1   Choose something to talk about that you are both familiar with. For instance, how you spent last weekend *or* your day so far *or* your part-time job.

STAGE 2 Start talking – both at the same time. Concentrate on what you are saying. Keep this up for two minutes.

STAGE 3 This time **A** starts talking. The moment **A** hesitates or stops, **B** starts talking. **A** listens for a pause and then talks again, picking up exactly where he/she left off. And so on.

Interviews for magazines and television

A reporter for a magazine article or a host on a television show must find the right questions to bring out the best in the person being interviewed.

STAGE 1 *Work in groups of four.* The questions an interviewer asks are important if he/she is to obtain interesting material. Compare these two extracts from interviews by pupils and decide which would make the better interview. Give reasons.

Interview A

Mark	How old are you?
Annette	Fifteen.
Mark	What school do you go to?
Annette	St Andrew's Comprehensive.
Mark	What do you want to do when you leave?
Annette	I dunno really. I haven't made up my mind.
Mark	What TV programmes do you like?
Annette	Serials … things that go on from week to week.
Mark	What do you do in the evening?
Annette	Watch telly, meet my friends, make my own clothes …

Interview B

Cheryl	If you were given a thousand pounds, what would you spend it on?
Wayne	A diving suit and diving equipment.
Cheryl	Diving? Are you interested in that?
Wayne	Yes, very, ever since I was about ten.
Cheryl	Do you go diving?
Wayne	Only in the local baths. I'm training, you see. I'm not allowed to go diving in rivers or the sea until I'm proficient and can

Cheryl interviewing Wayne

stay under water for five minutes. I've not used a tank yet –
that comes later. I just use a snorkel.

Cheryl   How long can you stay under with a tank?

Wayne   Till the oxygen runs out, about half an hour.

STAGE 2   *Work in pairs.*

1   Make a list of interesting questions together. (You will need a copy
each.) Remember that questions like
    'What are the things you hate most of all?'
    'What famous person would you like to meet and talk to?'
    'What are you most frightened of?'
are likely to arouse more interest than
    'How do you spend your evenings?'
    and 'Where do you live?'

2   Find a new partner.

3   Take it in turns to interview each other, using your list of questions
as a framework. Adapt your questions and add to them when
appropriate. For instance, if you find a topic which interests your
partner, follow it through as Cheryl did, otherwise your interview
will sound superficial and uninteresting. An interview is only as
good as the interviewer.

STAGE 3 *Recording your interview*
EITHER
Tape the interview. Play it back for the rest of the class to comment on.
OR
Write up your interview material as a magazine article (about 350 words). Your article will sound more lively if you use quotations and if you include your own impressions of the person you are interviewing. Before you start, read the short interview below, written by a girl of your age, and use it as a guide.

<u>An interview with Jane</u>

'Ooh, I love Chinese take-aways!' Jane burst out as I asked her what her favourite food was. She obviously enjoyed eating. She liked spicy food but had never tried Indian as her parents didn't much like it. The most interesting food she has ever eaten is frogs' legs which she said were lovely.

'My dad once brought some winkles in vinegar back from a shop but I couldn't taste them as I'm allergic to vinegar.'

If she didn't have to learn the new language, the country Jane would most like to live in is Africa, or the Middle East.

'America sounds nice too but I'm not as keen on that as much as Africa.'

She is not afraid of bombs or terrorists in Africa and would like to live on a safari in Kenya. She likes all animals, and is not afraid of snakes or spiders.

'I find tarantulas interesting and even water hogs have some appeal!'

STAGE 4 Pin all the interviews to your noticeboard. Read them and discuss whose was the best and why.

A television interview

Work in pairs.
Read this extract in which Terry Wogan interviews Michael Palin.

Wogan   Let's have a breath of good old British pluck and poise and sanity. Who better than the refugee from the Monty Python home for the bewildered, former lumberjack and parrot salesman, ladies and gentlemen, Michael Palin! . . . . . . You're known – it may be a description you reject – as the most sane of the Pythons.

Palin   Yes – bit like being described as the least violent of the Kray twins, you know. Erm, amongst that mob you know, where is sanity? We're all a bit off our bottle. But, er, I think all the Pythons have this sort of way of putting the lid on rather tightly but underneath the surface we're all absolute lunatics.

Wogan   Not so far beneath the surface! . . . . . . You're – you're chairman – I can't imagine how – of Transport 2000, a pressure group for the improvement of public transport. How did you get that job?

Palin   Well I was complaining on Leeds station very bitterly about British Rail and, er – someone – someone was there listening to my moans and suddenly I thought 'My God, he's the chairman of British Rail!' 'cos he was trying to defend them rather stoutly. It turned out he was someone who knew of the Transport 2000 group and what I was saying really was that I am a great fan of trains, I love trains, I wished they would work better. He said, 'Well, why don't you join Transport 2000 which is a group which tries to make public transport work better' and I thought that was a laudable aim and so I sort of lent them my name in the hope of – of – you know . . .

Wogan   It – it's just trains, is it? What about the lot of – say – the simple cyclist?

Palin   No, it's the whole lot actually – simple cyclists, pedestrians. It's really all travellers I suppose, I mean, motorists as well. I mean, Transport 2000's idea is that – that transport should be more coordinated and should work better – you know – cars will move faster, trains go better and buses go faster – you know – if, er, routes were more carefully planned.

Wogan   Does the committee treat you as a chairman should be – with dignity – or do they start telling you jokes?

Palin

Palin   No, no, I tell *them* jokes. We do have hilarious board
meetings. No it's really quite a serious thing – about nineteen
or twenty people attend the board meeting, representing all
the various kinds of travellers. I found it incredibly interesting
'cos I tend to think, oh, trains are late, buses are late – there's
nothing I can do but there is a bit you can do and a lot of
people have alternatives – sensible alternatives – to sitting
in traffic jams all day.

STAGE 1   Discuss these questions:

What indications are there that Michael Palin is speaking spon-
taneously without a script?

What words does Palin use which you would not find in a written
account of an interview? Why does Palin need to use these words?

How does Wogan develop the topic of Palin's chairmanship of 'Transport 2000'?

Why does Wogan say, 'I can't imagine how'?

STAGE 2   Prepare your television interview. **A** is the host and **B** is to be interviewed as him/herself. Choose the questions together. Questions like 'What is the most frightening thing that has happened to you?' will provide the most interesting answers. Rehearse your show together. **A** may join in the talk, but without dominating or interrupting **B**. Use this list of questions to help you.

What was your first memory?
What is your first school memory?
What was your favourite toy as a child?
What annoys you most?
What is your favourite colour?
Has one of your dreams ever come true?
What is your favourite sport?
What is your favourite group?
What are your strong points as a person?
What are your weak points as a person?
What is your favourite food?
What is your most unhappy memory?
What was your best holiday?
What is the funniest thing you can remember?
What is your favourite book?
Do you have a Saturday job?
Are you scared of anything?
What is the best film you have ever seen over the past year?

STAGE 3   Each pair take it in turns to present their television interview to the rest of the class. When all the pairs have been watched, the class may vote which host wins the EMMY award.

STAGE 4   Prepare another television interview. This time **B** is the host and **A** takes the role of a famous person he/she admires. You may have to do some research together in order to find enough material.

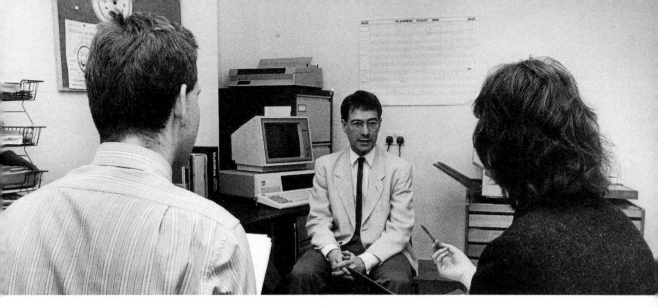

Interviewing with a purpose

So far we have looked at interviews designed to interest and entertain. If we do not like the person being interviewed, or make a wrong judgement, there is nothing lost. There are occasions, however, where it is vital that we ask the right questions and make the right judgement – interviews for jobs, or surveys of opinions, for instance.

Interviews for jobs

The message behind the words

STAGE 1 *Work in pairs*. Pupil **A** interviews pupil **B** in the following three ways for a Saturday job stocking shelves in a large supermarket.

1 **A** acts very high status – makes **B** wait for the interview; looks down on and tries to catch **B** out; picks on **B**'s weak points; and makes **B** feel small.
2 **A** acts very low status – loses paper; does not look **B** in the eye; hesitates; is apologetic.
3 **A** is smiling, encouraging; asks about **B**'s interests and strong points; tries to put **B** at ease.

Discussion
How did **B** react to these different interviews? What did he/she reveal about him/herself in movements of hands and feet? Which type of interviewer did **A** prefer to be? Why? What would each type of interview reveal about a candidate? Which is the best type of interview for finding out about the candidate?

Discussion What jobs
would you expect each of
these people to go for?
What influences your
choice? Are you being
prejudiced?

STAGE 2   The content of an interview

Work in groups of 3–5. There are certain requirements that all jobs have. What do you think they are? Can these be tested in an interview? You might find out whether a person is punctual or honest from references. What other qualities will you be looking for in an interview? Remember that it is no use asking 'Are you always on time?' because the candidate will simply reply, 'Yes.'

Is there any point in asking about the candidate's interests? What might this reveal to you? Is there any point asking about previous experience? Is it useful to discuss the candidate's qualifications?

Write down your final questions.

Interviews – a role-play

In this role-play you will be asked to hold interviews for choosing sixth formers for places on teacher training courses. This will give you practice in any kind of interview, but you probably have more ideas about what makes a good teacher, and therefore will have more to draw on from your own experience in the role-play.

You will play the part *either* of a member of the interviewing panel *or* a sixth former.

Initial discussion

Decide what qualities an interviewing panel is looking for in a potential teacher. What type of person would make a good teacher?

STAGE 1   Divide these roles between you.
— four or five pupils are the sixth formers;
— the remainder of the class divide into five interviewing panels, consisting of lecturers, and representing each of these colleges:

Hurlstone – set in beautiful countryside; plenty of opportunities for all kinds of sporting activities; accommodation provided for all students in modern purpose-built blocks; active students' union; nearest town five miles away; beaches two miles away.

Castra – very good academic record; 97% of fourth-year students obtained teaching posts; some accommodation; after first year, students must find their own accommodation; good students' union; site not particularly attractive but plenty of social activities.

Weston – small market town; good reputation for training students; caring; accommodation provided for all students; few sports activities,

but very strong music and drama clubs; students recommend the social life.

London – very little accommodation; students must find their own accommodation; very good social and cultural life in London itself, but expensive; lecturers young and enthusiastic.

St Paul's – two miles outside the town; buses run frequently; very good science facilities; modern, purpose-built accommodation.

STAGE 2   For the sixth-form candidates

When you apply for a course to train to be a teacher, you must complete an application form. Invent details according to the character you wish to play. Write out the answers to this form, under the numbered headings. Do not mark this book.

1	SURNAME FIRST NAMES		ADDRESS	
2	Sex Date of birth Age in years and months Country of birth Nationality			

3	**Choice of college in order of preference**			
	1		4	
	2		5	
	3			

4	**Education from age 11 in date order** Name and location of schools/colleges	from month/year	to month/year

5	**Details of employment to date, including part-time employment**			
	Names and addresses of employers	Nature of work	from month/year	to month/year

6	**Examinations for which results known**			
	Subject	Examination date month year	Level	Results

Notes for completion

Section 2 *Age* If you are a sixth former, you will be about 18 years old.

Section 3 *Choice of college* You may choose any order of preference from the colleges. Bear in mind that colleges you place towards the bottom of the list are less likely to look favourably on your application.

Examinations to be taken		
Subject	Examination date month year	Level

Subject(s) and age-range which candidate wishes to teach. Give reasons for choice.

Further information, hobbies, interests and experience relevant to application.

Confidential statement by referee

Name of referee
Post/occupation
Reference

Signed ....
Date ....

Section 5   You might want to invent a job dealing with children for this section, for instance running a playgroup.

Section 9   Again include some details which show you are interested in children.

Section 10 The college will want to know if the candidate is: honest, reliable, conscientious, a leader, punctual, hard-working, tactful with people, etc.

STAGE 3   ## For the five interviewing panels of lecturers

Instructions

1   Read through the information given on pages 24–5 about the colleges and negotiate with the other groups for the college you wish to work in.

2   Decide how you wish to interview:
   — Will you set the 'room' up very formally with the lecturers ranged along a table looking at the candidate, or informally in easy chairs with no tables?
   — Will you all be friendly, smiling, kindly? Or fire sharp questions to catch the candidate out? (A particularly unnerving practice is to walk up and down behind the candidate.) Or will you be a mixture – some of you friendly, some difficult?
   — Will one of you lead the interview?
   — What type of questions will you ask? For instance, if you are looking for someone who is hard-working and conscientious, it will not help you to ask:
      'Are you hard-working?'
   It might be better to ask:
      'Tell us how you spend your evenings.'
   The interview will be 10–15 minutes long, so make sure that you have enough questions to ask.

STAGE 4   1   The candidates give completed forms to the colleges to read. Colleges pass them round and note down any questions they now wish to ask.

2   Meanwhile, the candidates decide:
   — How will you enter the room?
   — How will you sit?
   — Will you smile?
   — How will you cope with difficult questions?
   — Will you look directly at the person you are talking to?
   — Will you tell the truth?

STAGE 5   ## The role-play

1   Colleges set up the interviewing rooms.
2   Candidates take back application form and go to the first college.
3   Interviews should be 10–15 minutes long. At the end of that time, the interview should be concluded and the candidate goes to the next college.

STAGE 6   The verdict

1   When all the interviews have been completed, *each college* discusses which candidate they want. Base your discussion on the personalities revealed in the interview.

2   *The candidates* discuss which college they would like to go to.

STAGE 7   Final discussion

As a class, discuss

i What you found interesting/difficult/easy in the role-play.

ii The reasons for your choices.

A consumer survey

When a company brings out a new product, it needs to find out what people want and what they will buy. It asks its market researchers to organise a survey to test public opinion. If the researchers receive the wrong impressions, great sums of money may be at stake. The researchers must consider the questions they ask very carefully.

STAGE 1   Read this scene in which the sales manager of a cosmetics company is asking his market researcher to test opinion about a new lipstick.

Manager   We've developed a new product – it's a lipstick that doesn't wear off after eating and drinking.

Researcher   Sounds an interesting idea. I'd buy it for a start. I get fed up feeling my lipstick fade during a business lunch and having to dive into the Ladies to touch it up. We'll do a survey for you, but it sounds very straightforward.

Manager   Ah well, it isn't as simple as that. The lipstick doesn't come off at all unless you also buy a little bottle of our specially developed lipstick remover. That's the drawback of our new product. Women may have a resistance to using remover on their lips, whereas they're used to removing eye make-up. Also it makes the package expensive – it'll cost twice as much as an average lipstick. And it'll take up more room in the make-up bag.

Researcher   I suppose you also want to know how many women do wear lipstick and how many more would if they knew it didn't rub off?

Manager   Yes – we do need to update our last survey on lipsticks. And we're also interested in the male market. With the arrival of punk and make-up for men, we want to know whether there's any interest there. Also we want to test men's general awareness of lipstick. Do they know what colour lipstick they like to see their women wear? I know it's a bit unlikely, but we want to know whether it's possible to get men to buy lipstick as a present for their women.

Researcher   It does sound unlikely. My husband hasn't a clue what lipstick I wear. But there's no harm in testing the market. Right, give me until next Friday and then I'll show you what I've come up with.

STAGE 2 *Work in pairs.* Make out a list of the information the sales manager wishes to find out.

STAGE 3 Draw up two lists of questions: one designed to test women's opinions; and one to test men's. About five questions each should be sufficient. More than that and you may make the consumer impatient or bored. Structure your question in such a way that they are easy to collect the answers: for instance,

1 (*to a man*) If it became fashionable, would you wear lipstick for men?	**Answer** Yes/No/Don't know

STAGE 4 *As a class*, compare your lists of questions. Which questions did you think were most useful? Why? What are the limitations of testing opinion by using a survey?

Your own survey

Imagine that your class has been asked to test whether pupils in your school would be interested in a uniform which would be more expensive but more fashionable. You wish to know:
a   What pupils feel generally about uniform.
b   Whether they thought a more expensive uniform would be unfair on those who could not pay for it.
c   Whether a more fashionable uniform would be silly because it would date.
d   Whether they think their parents would be interested in the idea.
e   Whether they agree about what is fashionable.
f   What preferences they have for colour and material.

STAGE 5 Draw up questions to find out this information. You may wish to spend a little time working in pairs and then pool your ideas as a class to create a final list.

STAGE 6 Interview pupils at break and lunchtime. Make sure that your sample is representative by interviewing an equal mix of boys, girls, ages, interests.

STAGE 7 Obtain your results by counting the number of Yes/No/Don't know answers you get for each question. What conclusions can you draw from your survey?

Discussion
What features in these old-fashioned uniforms have been retained today? Does this tell you anything about fashion in uniform?

*The role of **B** in Warm-up 1 on page 14*

You are dumb. You cannot speak and you cannot write. You can only nod and shake your head, *but* you will respond if the police officer says 'show me' or 'describe to me' either by miming or drawing the information.

Decide what you reply by answering these questions:

How many people were there?
What sex were they?
Did they have a car? What sort?
Did they carry any weapons?
Were they disguised?
How did they break into the shop?
What did they carry with them?
Where were you? What were you doing?
How did the group get away?

After five minutes you can volunteer the information – in *mime* – that one of the gang has a butterfly tattoo on left cheek.

2 Talking to people

This section looks at what you might like to tell people – stories, jokes, opinions, instructions, explanations. It also shows how talking requires someone to listen – and listen carefully.

You will be asked to:

- talk without hesitating
- persuade
- evaluate talks given by pupils
- prepare a talk
- present a talk
- tell a story
- add to a story
- evaluate a story told by a pupil
- consider the use of language in a spoken story
- compare a spontaneous and a polished version of a story
- examine the way a joke is constructed
- tell a joke
- give instructions
- demonstrate a skill
- evaluate your ability to give an instruction clearly
- describe
- demonstrate your ability to listen

Talking without hesitation

A talking game

Work in groups of 5.

Choose one person to time the talks and keep the score.

One person chooses one of the subjects below and gives a talk for 15 seconds.

Any of the rest of the group may challenge if the person hesitates or repeats him/herself. The time-keeper decides if the challenge is a correct one.

The challenger takes over the subject and talks for 15 seconds. Score two points for completing a talk.

Repeat until everyone has started a talk.

Repeat with 30-second talks and one-minute talks.

15-second talks	*30-second talks*	*one-minute talks*
Making toast	Spots	My last holiday
Making a cup of tea	Football hooligans	Taking the dog for a walk
Feeding the dog	Sunbathing	
Cleaning your teeth	Shoes	How to break dance
Toothache	Choosing clothes	The Post Office
Boiling an egg	Vacuuming the house/ flat	When I had to go to hospital
Feeling afraid		
Waking up	Bathing the baby	Delivering papers
Feeling ill	My walk to school	Saturday job
Autumn	The school bus	The film I saw last week
Apples	Digital watches	
Blisters	When I felt a fool	The biggest problem in Britain
Wearing glasses	Trains are better than buses	
Superman/Super- woman	Girls work harder than boys	Schools should teach more non-competi- tive sports
Video recorders	Santa Claus	All children should go to a comprehensive
The Moon	How I would improve school	
Sundays		Homework should be voluntary

Talking with persuasion

Making a sale

Work in pairs.

STAGE 1   **A** is a householder and sets up one or two chairs for the living-room, and to mark out the front door.

STAGE 2   **B** is a salesperson and chooses one of these to sell:

double glazing	watches
encyclopedias	greenhouses
perfumes	paintings
cleaning materials	shoes
jewellery	pottery
insurance	vacuum cleaners

Preferably everybody playing should sell something different.

STAGE 3   **B** knocks at **A**'s front door and attempts to make a sale. **A** should be polite but not willing to buy so that **B** does not have too easy a task.

Suggestions to help you

You are more likely to make a sale if you are polite, cheerful and flattering rather than aggressive and bullying.

You will want to make your way into **A**'s living room but you must not force your way in. It is better to say something like: 'That's a lovely picture! May I have a closer look at it?'

You must be ready to invent reasons why **A** might want your product.

STAGE 4   When you have made a sale, **B** finds a new partner to whom he/she tries to sell the product or service.

STAGE 5   After **B** has 'visited' 5 or 6 householders, **A** becomes the salesperson and sells to 5 or 6 new householders.

STAGE 6   *Discussion – as a class*
When you have completed this exercise, decide who you thought was the most successful at selling and why.

Talks about hobbies, interests, jobs

STAGE 1   Read these extracts from talks given by two fourth years.

Julie   I'm going to tell you about horses. Erm . . . er, I go every week to the stables in Houghton and I . . . er . . . clean the horses out and . . . I get a free ride for doing that. I like doing it. You er use a special brush for brushing the horse um . . . and you have to make sure it's clean. And then I muck the stables out. I don't mind that and er . . . Oh yes, before I go out on the ride I have to tack up. We take people out for about an hour round near the river.

Donna   Have you ever thought about who weighs up all those bags of nuts and dried fruit in the health food shop? Well, on Saturdays it's me. I started looking for a job – ooh – about a year ago now, but it was the only one I could get. It's funny really, because I don't like health food.
I spend all day weighing things into little plastic bags. I'm allowed to go over or under by – um – no more than half a gramme. It gets very boring and I'm not allowed to do anything else. But in about six weeks, Mr Ruston – he's my boss – he says I'll be ready to serve customers.

In pairs, discuss why you prefer one talk to the other.

STAGE 2 Preparing your talk

1 Choose a topic you feel comfortable with and which you know a good deal about. Do not try to be too ambitious at first.
2 Write out your talk in detail, either in note form or as an essay.
3 Check that you have a lively opening to seize your audience's attention. (Donna, for instance, began with a question.)
4 Check that your talk is not a list of random statements, like Julie's, but that you develop your points as Donna does.
5 When you have written your talk, summarise each paragraph or point in four or five words. Write these on a small card which you will have with you when you speak.
6 Make sure that you know your speech thoroughly. This will give you the confidence not to hesitate or stammer. However, do not repeat your speech parrot fashion, as there will be little life in it.
7 If you feel you lack confidence, use props which you can talk about. Julie, for instance, could have brought in some of the brushes etc. that she uses, and this would have given her talk a focus.

STAGE 3 Giving your talk

1 Breathe in and out slowly and deeply before you start. This will calm your nerves.
2 Smile and look directly at your audience.
3 Your notes should only be to remind you. Do not stare at them.
4 Put as much expression as you can into your voice and face.
5 Have the confidence to know that you are an interesting person. Remember: everyone else must give a talk as well!

Discussion What do you think these children and young people are listening to? How do you know?

Talks about politics, current affairs and issues

These need greater research and preparation than talks on your hobby or interests.

STAGE 1   *In pairs*, compare the openings of these two talks:

Peter   I think a tunnel to France would be a good idea 'cos um . . . 'cos . . . it would be cheaper to go abroad. But then it would make the ferries go bankrupt. While it's being built, it would . . . er . . . mean a lot of employment. It wouldn't be much cheaper than the ferry – but it . . . er . . . depends which way they do it.

Ali   People have wanted a tunnel for nearly a hundred years now. It makes sense to have one when we are in the EEC and looking to Europe for our trade. It will make transporting freight much easier, apart from . . . er . . . speeding up the journey if you're going on holiday abroad by car. You know what it's like – sitting at Dover for an hour and a half and then an uncomfortable ride in a boat getting seasick if it gets too rough.

   Is the tunnel a good idea? The fact that people have been thinking about it so long shows . . . er . . . that . . . um . . . that there are problems. Now we have the technology to overcome these problems.

Decide which is the better talk. Give your reasons.

STAGE 2   **Planning your talk**

1   Choose an area that you already know something about – either from newspapers, or from a book you have read; otherwise you will find yourself like Peter, with little to say.
2   Research the facts that you need for your talk. Study newspapers or look in your reference library. Do not copy wholesale but make brief notes of what you have read.
3   Plan your talk point by point. One way is to write down lots of questions and then answer them. Then put them in a logical order.
4   Write out your talk and then write out brief summarising notes on a small card. Check that your talk is organised logically.
5   Do not cram your talk with facts. Your audience can only absorb so much. Make it more interesting by including your opinion and relevant stories you know, as Ali has done by briefly describing the sea-crossing.
6   Make sure you have a lively opening, to seize your audience's attention.

How are these speakers using their hands and faces to help them?

Make up a thirty-second speech to fit one of these speakers. Practise your speech, using their expressions and gestures to help you.

STAGE 3 Giving your talk

The advice is the same as that for the talk on your hobby (see page 38). Be especially careful to speak slowly so that your audience can absorb the information.

A choice of topic

Here are some suggestions and starting points for you to choose from. Or you may choose your own.

You are what you eat
Medical evidence that high-fat, low-fibre diet is unhealthy; obesity a feature of modern life; should additives be banned? Should you be free to choose your own diet? Are there arguments for not eating meat? Do people who live on junk foods look more unhealthy?

Home videos – the case for and against
Do videos make people lazy? How have they affected the cinema? Do you watch what you record or are you always leaving programmes for a rainy day? Is there anything worth recording on television? Are the more violent films unsuitable/dangerous for children to watch?

Public versus private transport
Are cars ruining our environment? Are they economical? Convenient? What about people living in rural areas? What about old people? Should public transport be cheap and plentiful? Would people use it if it were? Should families own two cars? Should freight be transported by train or lorry?

Modern farming
Are farmers ruining our countryside by putting more land under the plough? Have they a responsibility to manage the land by planting trees and hedges? Should they be allowed to spray crops with chemical fertilisers? What are the latest developments in farming technology? What effect will they have?

Unemployment
Has Government a responsibility to provide jobs? Is unemployment a greater problem for young or middle-aged people? How does being unemployed damage a person? What kinds of jobs are disappearing? What kind of jobs are appearing in their place? What are the prospects twenty years from now?

Police relations and public order
Should the police improve their community image? How do different sections of the community view the police? What powers do the police

need? What powers do they have? What should happen if they abuse these powers? Is confidence in the police important? Is a police force necessary in society? How did it develop?

Animals and experiments
Should animals be used to test cosmetics? To test drugs and medicine? To research into cancer, heart trouble and other diseases? Are the violent actions of the Animal Rights campaigners justified? Is keeping pets cruel? What rights have human beings over animals?

Telling a story

Suzanne told this story about a school French trip to her classmates, without preparation.

When we went to La Baule last summer, right, we were going with Mrs Acres and Mrs Long and we all know how strict Mrs Acres is and what a strop Mrs Long is, so we were sort of quite dreading it and we found out on the holiday that Mrs Acres was having a right strop at everything as we thought and Mrs Long didn't raise her voice once and she was really nice.

It was all right till we were coming home. As you can – can probably see, Mrs Long has – has problems with her walking – she's got funny feet in other words – and she had these really heavy bags right, and Mrs Acres – we had put them on this trolley right and um we piled as many as we could on the trolley but we couldn't get them all on and when we went back, Mrs Acres said 'What about all these ones?' and we said there wasn't enough room on the trolley so she made us get another trolley and take them, and then Mrs Long carried Mrs Acres' bag for her. She was going on saying 'Carry these bags, carry these bags, carry my bags.' So Mrs Long ended up carrying Mrs Acres' bags for miles with her sore feet and all and afterwards I says casually to Mrs Acres: 'Oh, by the way, Mrs Long carried your bags all the way,' and she just said, 'Oh yes, so you did, thank you, Mrs Long.'

Anyway, we all had to rush to the station while Mrs Acres got a taxi and Mrs Long walked and Mrs Long has got problems with her feet and we all thought that was pretty unfair. Anyway, right, we got to the train station and I was holding Mrs Acres' handbag right, a bag, and it was really heavy 'cos I was carrying my bag, and it hurt 'cos I'd sunburn and all blisters all over my back. So I was carrying Mrs Acres' bag but unbeknown to me it had two bottles of wine in it. I was pretty fed up and I got this bag and I said to Paul, 'Catch, Paul,' and I threw it at Paul and he sort of missed and it went flip and it went on to the floor and the bottles of wine smashed. It was really funny, right, and Paul went white – he was so worried – and when Mrs Acres came along, we said, 'Miss, the bottles are broken. We don't know *how* it happened. We just put them down and it came leaking out.'

She said, 'And I was just going to give them to the nice man who arranged this trip.'

And Mrs James she'd lost her purse, right, and – what was it? – all her credit cards, all her money and Mrs Acres was bothered about these bottles of flaming wine. She was going, 'Oh my bottles of wine, I was going to give them to that poor man.'

Analysis

Work in pairs.

1　Make a list of the words in Suzanne's speech which are used in informal speech not in formal writing.
2　What function do these words have in speech?
　　anyway　sort of　right　and
3　This story was told without preparation. How might the teller improve it, if she had time to think about it first?

Your own story

STAGE 1　Choose an incident that happened to you or that you saw happen and which you found memorable, either because it was, for instance, sad, funny, annoying, embarrassing.

STAGE 2　*In pairs*, each takes it in turns to tell the other about the incident, without any preparation. If you can, tape the stories.

STAGE 3　Comment on each other's work. Suggest ways of improving your partner's story.

STAGE 4　Take it in turns to tell the class your story. If you can, tape the stories.

STAGE 5　If you have taped the stories, compare your unprepared with your polished story.

Accent

Most people speak with at least some traces of the area in which they were born, or where they have lived for most of their lives. An accent can improve the telling of a story, especially if the story belongs to a particular region or a particular group of people.

Betsy White spent her childhood among the 'travelling people' in Scotland. This is one of the stories she heard round the camp fires when the caravans were all drawn together for the night.

If the class has no Scottish person to read the story, then two or three people might attempt it in a Scottish accent.

One day my granny said to my mother, are you coming with me?, she says, see if we get anything for your supper. And they went on the road and on the road but they couldn't see a thing, not a thing. And they wandered and wandered till it was nearly dark. So my granny says well I . . . you'll go hungry to bed tonight . . . She says there's only one place, she said, that's about a mile further up the glen. There's a young shepherd's wife up here and she never lets me awa' without gieing me something. She says do you think you'd be able to walk up. Och aye, my mother says, I'll easily manage to walk up wi' you. So they're walking up the road and my granny said you'll maybe see a wee baby when you go up here, she said, because the last time I was at this lassie she was expecting a baby. So that'll please you if you see a wee baby. She says aye. But anyway, when they got to the door and my granny knocked at the door, this young woman come out and she looked terrible. Her eyes were sunk in the back of her head, and there was nothing but the skin covering the bones, and she was really bad looking. But my granny didna want to afear the lassie so she just said are ye all right lassie? Oh well she says, not too bad. She says did you have a bad birth? No she says, I didna have a bad birth, but I've got an awfully bad bairn. Och awa', my granny says, there's nae such thing as a bad bairn. Well this one is a bad bairn, she said. Listen to him. And my granny could hear this bairn whingeing and greeting and carrying on inside. She said, but come in Maggie and take a look at him. And my granny come in and this bairn was lying kicking and screaming and kicking and carrying on, and granny says does he ever shed any tears? No, no, she says, there's never any tears, just this greeting and carrying on all the time. But never mind Maggie, she said, come on into the shed and I'll give you a poke of tatties to take home to the bairns. And she said to my mother will you rock the cradle 'til we come back. My mother says och aye, I'll rock the cradle. So she was standing there rocking this cradle. Now this bairn was only a month old but it got up and stuck its tongue out at her, stood on its hands you see like this, and stuck out its tongue. So she's out the door like a shot and run to this lean-to shed where the two women were. And she whispered in Gaelic — that's the traveller's ain language — to my granny. So my granny looked at her, and the woman says what is she saying? Oh, she's asking if you have a toilet about this place. Aye, bairn, she says, down the thick of the garden there's a toilet in there. So my mother ran doon there, and the two women went back into the house, and my granny had another look at this bairn, you see. She says, you ken lassie, I think I could cure your bairn. I see you've still got you're old bike there in the shed. She said if you jump on your bike and go doon to the village and get a wee muskin of whisky and a wee jar of honey, she says, and bring it back to me I'll cure your bairn. She says that's if you have enough to get it wi'. Oh, Maggie, she says, I'll get it even if I have to borrow it if you think it's going to make any difference to him. She said I've tried everything and the nurse has tried everything. Ah well you just awa' and do that, my granny says. Now as soon as my granny got the woman awa', and watched her out of sight down the road, she shouted to my mother: come here lassie, she says, run and get me a shovelful of horse's dung. She says get that big shovel, it's in the shed out there, and fill it full and bring it in to me. So my mother says what do you want with horse's dung? Never mind asking any questions, she says, just go and do as you're telled. So my mother went to and she got this ... there was nae problem getting a shovelful of your horse's dung at that time, and she brought it back in. So my granny put it down on the floor, then she lifted this bairn out of the cradle — he was still howling and whingeing, and put him sitting on top of the horse dung. Then she lifted this shovel of horse dung and put it on top of this peat fire and she held it there, and my mother started to howl and roar and scream, oh ma, ma, what ha'e ye did with the woman's bairn. I'm no' that hungry, ma, stop it! stop it! She said, awa' ye go lassie, awa' ye go, she says, I ken what I'm doing, she says. Oh ma, she says, stop it. She thought her mother had taken a mad turn or something. But anyway she held that bairn until the shovel got red hot, then this bairn, instead of screaming and whingeing and greeting, it started to curse and swear in the Gaelic, and it cursed and swore and cursed and swore, but my granny held it and held it on the fire, till all of a sudden it went phui! up the lum[1] in a puff of reek. But then my mother says oh ma, the bairn's back in the cradle, and she says is it? She says that's fine. She says the bairn's back in the cradle, but that was nae the bairn that went up the lum. She says but come and help me to clean up this mess 'cos it was all soot and earth and everything. So they hurried up and tidied up and the house before the young mother come back. And she come in and she says, don't tell me that he's quiet. Aye, he's quiet now, my granny said. Did you get what I telled you? Aye, the lassie said, here ye are. So my granny took, och, about two drops of the whisky and about a quarter of a teaspoonful of the honey and a wee drop more of water and she mixed them up and lifted the bairn and fed it to it. She says there now, there's your bairn and I don't think you'll hae anymair bother wi' it.

[1] lum – chimney

Discussion

Work in pairs.
What words and phrases show the story to be in Scottish dialect?
Why is it a suitable story for telling in a strong accent?

A story in your own accent

In pairs, prepare a story in the accent of your own area, or one you are familiar with. Try to choose a story that is particularly suitable for the accent, perhaps an old one you might have heard from your grandparents, or one about a local incident or legend.

Either tape your story for the class to hear, or take turns to tell your story to the rest of the class.

Discussion

Look at the pictures on the next page. How do the storytellers use their bodies and faces in telling their tale?

Giving precise instructions

Warm up 1

*Work in pairs; label yourselves **A** and **B**.* You will both need paper and pen.

STAGE 1 Sit back to back. **A** draws a simple geometric shape which **B** must not see.

STAGE 2 **A** describes the shape to **B** in *words* for **B** to draw on his/her paper.

STAGE 3 When you have finished, compare drawings.

STAGE 4 **B** draws a more complicated shape, perhaps with curves, and exchanges the drawing with another **B**.

STAGE 5 Sitting back to back, **B** describes the new shape he/she has been given to **A** who draws it.

STAGE 6 Compare drawings and discuss the problems which arose and the reasons for any inaccuracies.

Warm up 2

*Work in pairs; label yourselves **A** and **B**.*

STAGE 1 **B** removes his/her jacket, coat or jumper.

STAGE 2 **A** instructs **B** *using words only* how to put the article back on.

STAGE 3 **A** removes an article of clothing and **B** instructs.

STAGE 4 Discuss the difficulties which arose. Did you find the right words to convey what you meant?

Giving a demonstration

Demonstrate one of these to your class. Use mime or objects and the board to help you as necessary.

How to
— knit
— mend a bike puncture
— wire a 13 amp plug
— give mouth to mouth resuscitation
— ski
— play and land a large fish

— type
— bath a baby
— make and cook a pancake
— draw a face

After each demonstration, the class comments on how clear the instructions were.

You be the teacher

Your teachers give you different instructions constantly. Do they always make themselves clear? If an instruction fails to be carried out, how much is their fault for not making themselves clear, and how much is yours for not listening carefully enough?

STAGE 1   *Work in groups of 5–6.* **A** is the teacher and chooses one of these situations. Invent any extra details you need.

1   A PE teacher explaining the rules of football/rugby/cricket/netball/hockey. Ask the class to practise basic moves.
2   A Maths teacher explaining how to find the area of a triangle.
3   A computer teacher explaining the features of a BBC Micro.
4   Giving instructions about the arrangements for the last day of term.
5   Giving information about the procedure for fire drill.
6   Explaining what may or may not be worn to school.

STAGE 2   **A** asks the group questions to test whether they listened carefully and whether the instructions were clear.

STAGE 3   Each member of the group takes a turn at being teacher. Question the group after you have instructed them.

3 Read it aloud

To read well you have to

- understand what you are reading
- be clear and audible
- stress the right words
- read at the right pace (you would read a set of instructions more slowly than a dramatic story)
- find the right tone and manner

In this section you are asked to

- consider and experiment with various tones and expressions of voice
- practise an ironic tone
- practise reading poems solo, in pairs, and as a class
- evaluate your performance
- practise short dialogues
- look at how to enliven dialogue in stories
- attempt a formal reading of minutes
- read out a piece of information
- read out news items
- make up and read out your own news bulletins
- evaluate your own and others' newsreading

Your tone of voice

Work in pairs.

STAGE 1 When you speak and write, you use words. But when you speak you convey what you feel about those words by your tone of voice and your facial expressions. Exclamations like 'Oh!' 'Ah!' 'Well!' and 'Really!' have no meaning in themselves. How you say them is important.

Practise saying the exclamations to communicate these feelings. Use your face as well as your tone of voice.

surprise   sadness   despair   greed
anger   happiness   laziness   boredom

STAGE 2 Learn this piece of dialogue. **A** is waiting outside the cinema for **B** who is late.

B   Hello.
A   Hello.
B   Have you been waiting long?
A   Ages.
B   Have you bought the tickets?
A   No, I was waiting for you. It's your turn to pay.
B   Is it really?

STAGE 3 When you are familiar with the dialogue, try it out in as many different ways as you can think of. Here are some interpretations:

1   **A** is angry and **B** is apologetic about being late.
2   **A** is angry and **B** cheerfully ignores **A**'s feelings.
3   **A** is shy and almost apologetic about being early. Whereas **B** does not feel in the least to blame.
4   Both **A** and **B** are apologetic and shy.

STAGE 4 Choose one of your interpretations and perform it to your class. Ask them to identify what each of you was feeling and to give their reasons.

STAGE 5 When we use expressions like 'I've only got one pair of hands' or 'You've got eyes, haven't you?', we are stating one thing but meaning a great deal more.

Improvise five short scenes between a parent and a child (about 30 seconds each) around each of these lines. Make sure that your tone of voice brings out their full meaning.

'I've only got one pair of hands '
'You've got eyes, haven't you?'
'Have I got to wait all day!'

'I'd like to know what you mean by that.'
'Where do you think you are going?'

Showing how you feel

STAGE 1   *In pairs*, practise saying these expressions in the ways suggested.
Comment on each other's attempts.

'Thank you very much.'
— as if you really meant it
— as if you were being ironic
— as if you were leaving a shop

'That's nice.'
— in an enthusiastic way
— in a sarcastic way
— in an off-hand, casual way

'I don't know.'
— as if you weren't very interested
— as if you were puzzled
— as if you were angry at being asked

'Don't you?'
— in a threatening way
— in an off-hand way
— in a surprised way

STAGE 2   *In pairs*, learn this dialogue and say it as if **A** is accusing and **B** is
apologetic.

A   Did you do it?
B   No.
A   Why not?
B   I just didn't feel like it.
A   Well, when are you going to do it?
B   I don't know.
A   Soon?
B   Yes, as soon as I can.

STAGE 3   Now say it as if **A** is polite and **B** is irritable.

STAGE 4   Choose one interpretation to say in front of the class. Can they identify
which one you have chosen?

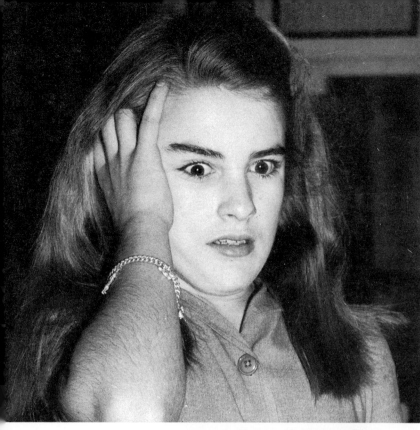

Write a 30-second dia-
logue you might have
with one of these people.

Clear speaking – reading with meaning

Sound your consonants

When you are speaking to an audience, particularly an audience of people who do not know you, you have a responsibility to make yourself audible to them. Many people do not normally sound their consonants (for example, *g* or *t* at the end of a word – goin*g*, hi*t*, or *tt* in the middle – pre*tt*y.) You must, however, exaggerate your consonants if you are speaking to an audience.

Practise this poem by enjoying and exaggerating the consonant sounds.

The Wendigo

> The Wendigo,
> The Wendigo!
> Its eyes are ice and indigo!
> Its blood is rank and yellowish!
> Its voice is hoarse and bellowish!
> Its tentacles are slithery,
> And scummy,
> Slimy,
> Leathery!
> 10   Its lips are hungry blubbery,
> And smacky,
> Sucky,
> Rubbery!
>
> The Wendigo,
> The Wendigo!
> I saw it just a friend ago!
> Last night it lurked in Canada;
> Tonight, on your veranada!
> As you are lolling hammockwise
> 20   It contemplates you stomachwise.
> You loll,
> It contemplates,
> It lollops.
> The rest is merely gulps and gollops.

Ogden Nash

A dramatic poem

The catch

You'll receive a
Vauxhall Viva
if you win our
competition:

oh, well done, sir,
you have won, sir,
here's the keys to
the ignition:

off you go now,
10 take it slow, now,
MIND OUR WALL –
oh dear, a skid, sir:

what a spill, sir,
here's our bill, sir:
you owe *us*
a thousand quid, sir!

Kit Wright

Solo work
In order to bring the story of the poem to life you will need to think
about these questions.

1 Who are you?
2 In what tone of voice do you say the first verse?
3 How do you speak to the winner in the second verse?
4 What tone do you use for
    'off you go now
    take it slow, now,'?
5 What do the capital letters tell you about how you should say –
    'MIND OUR WALL –'?
6 How should you say 'oh dear, a skid, sir' to make it sound funny?
7 What do the italics tell you about how you should say
    '*you* owe *us*
    a thousand quid, sir!'?

Learn the poem; your performance will be much improved.

A dialogue

Rabbiting On

Where did you go?
Oh ... nowhere much.

What did you see?
Oh ... rabbits and such.

Rabbits? What else?
Oh ... a rabbit hutch.

What sort of rabbits?
What sort? Oh ... small.

What sort of hutch?
10 *Just a hutch, that's all.*

But what did it look like?
Like a rabbit hutch.

Well, what was in it?
Small rabbits and such.

I worried about you.
While you were gone.

*Why don't you stop
Rabbiting on?*

Kit Wright

In pairs, discuss these questions about the poem before you start practising it. It is short enough for you to learn by heart.

1 Who do you think is saying the first line and who the second line of each verse? How will this affect your performances?
2 The first speaker asks a series of questions. In what tone should this person ask the first three or four questions? How should the tone change in the next verses?
3 What tone should be used for:
     'I worried about you
     While you were gone'?
4 What tone should the second speaker (in *italics*) use for the replies?
5 What tone should be used for:
     'Why don't you stop
     Rabbiting on?'?
   Will it be said quietly? Loudly? Irritatedly?
6 Will you both stand? Or sit? How will you stand/sit?

Dialects for comic effect

Framed in a First-storey Winder

Framed in a first-storey winder of a burnin' buildin'
Appeared: A Yuman Ead!
'Jump into this net, wot we are 'oldin'
And yule be quite orl right!'

But 'ee wouldn't jump ...

And the flames grew 'igher and 'igher and 'igher.
    (Phew!)

Framed in a second-storey winder of a burnin' buildin'
10 Appeared: A Yuman Ead!
'Jump into this net, wot we are 'oldin'
And yule be quite orl right!'

But 'ee wouldn't jump ...

And the flames grew 'igher and 'igher and 'igher.
    (Strewth!)

Framed in a third-storey winder of a burnin' buildin'
Appeared: A Yuman Ead!
'Jump into this net, wot we are 'oldin'
20 And yule be quite orl right!
Honest!'

And 'ee jumped ...

And 'ee broke 'is bloomin' neck!

Anon

Work in pairs.
Prepare for reading the poem by discussing these questions first.
Decide which of you will be the narrator.

1 What dialect is the poem written in?
2 How long will you pause in gaps between the verses or lines? What
   is the effect of these pauses?
3 For the narrator. Decide what tone you should use for these lines:
     'A Yuman Ead!' (Note the exclamation mark)
     'But 'ee wouldn't jump ...' (Will you say it differently the
     second time?)

'And the flames grew 'igher and 'igher and 'igher.' (Do you
raise your voice?)
'And 'ee broke 'is bloomin' neck!'
4   For the person giving the instructions:
Do you shout them? Do you cup your mouth?
Do you say the lines differently each time?
How should you say: 'Honest!'?

Reading an ambiguous poem

Song

Sylvia the Fair, in the bloom of Fifteen
Felt an innocent warmth, as she lay on the green;
She had heard of a pleasure, and something she guessed
By the towzing[1] and tumbling and touching her Breast:
She saw the men eager, but was at a loss,
What they meant by their sighing and kissing so close;
    By their praying and whining,
    And clasping and twining,
    And panting and wishing,
10   And sighing and kissing,
    And sighing and kissing so close.

Ah she cry'd, ah for a languishing Maid
In a Country of Christians to die without aid;
Not a Whig[2], or a Tory, or Trimmer[3] at least,
Or a Protestant Parson or Catholick Priest,
To instruct a young Virgin that is at a loss
What they meant by their sighing and kissing so close:
    By their praying and whining,
    And clasping and twining,
20   And panting and wishing,
    And sighing and kissing,
    And sighing and kissing so close.

Cupid in Shape of a Swayn[4] did appear,
He saw the sad wound, and in pity drew near,
Then showed her his Arrow, and bid her not fear,
For the pain was no more than a Malden may bear;
When the balm was infused, she was not at a loss
What they meant by their sighing and kissing so close,

By their praying and whining,
30   And clasping and twining,
And panting and wishing,
And sighing and kissing,
And sighing and kissing so close.

John Dryden

[1] towzing – make hair untidy
[2] Whig – a Liberal
[3] Trimmer – someone who changes political party, normally to join party in power; turncoat
[4] Swayn – lover

Work in mixed groups of 3 or 4.
Answer these questions to help you with the poem.

1   The poem is funny because it is deliberately ambiguous. What words will you emphasise to bring out this ambiguity?
2   The chorus tells of the desperation of the young men who are in love with Sylvia. How will you say the lines in order to bring out the comedy in the situation?
3   The second verse is Sylvia herself who cannot understand the fact that the figures of authority – politicians and priests – will not explain the situation to her! How should this verse be said in order to bring out her innocence and naïvety?
4   How will you divide the lines amongst you? Will one person play Sylvia? Another the narrator? Two more the young men?

Your own poem

Either solo or in pairs, choose a poem that you like and practise it. When you are ready, perform it in front of the rest of the class.

A formal reading

Committee meetings

In order to record opinions and decisions, the secretary of a committee takes minutes. These are read out at the next meeting as a reminder.

Work in pairs.
Read these minutes of the Beaconfield Youth Club clearly and slowly to each other. Comment on how clear your partner was.

The minutes

The minutes of a meeting of the committee of Beaconfield Youth Club held at the Club on the 20th September, 1986 at 7 p.m. Members present were: Asif, John, Zahida, Martin, Tom, Maureen and Mr Norman, the Club Leader. There were apologies for absence from Riphet and Amanda.

Mr Norman opened the meeting by reading the financial report for the year ending April 1986 which was approved.

A resolution to increase the Club subscription by £1 proposed by Asif was defeated. An amendment to increase it by 50p by John was passed.

Maureen suggested some 'I have paid my subscription' badges were bought. The cost of this was being looked into.

Mr Norman again raised the problem of chewing gum on the table-tennis and snooker tables. He read a letter out from Mrs Ellis, the cleaner, who said she would resign unless something was done about cleanliness and vandalism. After a long discussion a sub-committee of Asif, Tom and Zahida was formed to discuss ways of getting across to members the need to look after their own club.

An outing to Skegness for Easter Monday of 1987 was planned. It was decided that each member on booking must pay a half-share deposit.

Martin proposed that in future all club teams should be picked by the captain and the vice-captain and not just the captain. Some members felt that they were being left out by personal prejudice. After discussion it was felt that lack of fixtures was partly to blame, not giving enough members an opportunity to represent the club.

There being no further business the meeting closed at 9.15 p.m.

Work in pairs.

Write the minutes for a meeting of one of these organisations. Invent the details.

a youth club   The Ghost Hunting Club
The Hunt Saboteurs   The Charity Fund Raising Club

In pairs, take it in turns to read out the minutes. Comment on each other's performance.

Reading a piece of information

Solo work

Unlikely inventions

Practise reading the items below from John Craven's 'Newsround'. Follow this advice.

1   The items are meant to amaze or surprise us. Therefore when you read them aloud you will emphasise the unusual or surprising parts. Decide which words you will put most emphasis on.
2   Make a long pause after a full stop and a shorter one after a comma so your listeners can absorb the information.
3   How should you read the words written in *italics?*
4   The third item ends with a question. What tone of voice will you use?

Remarkable invention stories reach us frequently: this one comes from Russia. It's a pair of boots with a big difference. Each boot contains a small petrol engine. And the motors transmit so much power to the soles of the feet that whoever wears them can stride along in giant three-metre steps – that's at least three times bigger than normal. But Russian pedestrians aren't likely to rush off for a pair – the boots weigh almost six kilos, and you have to carry a can of petrol to keep them going. So they're not even as effective as seven-league boots in old fairy tales.

For those people who long to see themselves as others see them, an unusual product went on sale in America. It was called a Rorrim – that's mirror spelt backwards. Unlike ordinary mirrors, the rorrim shows a true reflection and doesn't reverse the image. So when you comb your hair, your parting on the left-hand side, appears on the right in the rorrim. And what's more, when you turn the rorrim upside down, it shows *you* upside down. Very confusing!

And from Finland comes news of an invention to please animal lovers. It's a painless mousetrap, and it took its inventor *thirty years* to work out. The trap looks like a box, and if a mouse touches the bait it will drop through a trapdoor, unharmed, into a cell below. The only trouble with this invention is that no one has suggested what you should *do* with the mouse once it was caught. Perhaps in another thirty years the inventor will provide the answer?

Here is the News

Newsreaders on television and radio read out written news reports. Originally they read very formally with no trace of individuality. But over the last ten years the style of reading has become more relaxed and varies a little according to the content of the news item and the reader's character.

STAGE 1 *In pairs*, make a list of the qualities you think television companies are looking for when they recruit newsreaders. What accent is required? How much individuality is allowed?

STAGE 2 *In pairs*, practise reading this news item. Imitate the style of a news-reader you have heard. How does the tone and the choice of words indicate that it is intended to be a light-hearted item?

Prince Andrew and Sarah Ferguson

Newsreader   The announcement of the engagement between Prince Andrew and Miss Sarah Ferguson is tonight believed to be imminent. There's nothing official but experts in these matters believe that all the signs are there. It's thought that Miss Ferguson had lunch with the Queen at Buckingham Palace. Andrew was out at a sporting engagement. Today Miss Ferguson went to work as normal but then met her father for lunch. So, as our court correspondent Michael Cole reports, the signs are that Buckingham Palace is laying the ground for the announcement of the couple's engagement.

Michael Cole Her day started quietly enough, driving through the mist from her family home in Hampshire to London all alone but with a reminder of Prince Andrew constantly in front of her – the little silver owl mascot on the bonnet given to her by the Prince because it's said he regards her as a beautiful nightbird who enjoys a real hoot. By the time she got to the office, accompanied by a colleague, the reporters were in tow to get any hint confirmed of their already published predictions that today was to be *the* day.

It wasn't of course, or she wouldn't have been going to work. But as always, she was charming while revealing nothing.

Lunch at Claridge's, the Royal Family's favourite hotel where the Queen held a party after the last Royal Wedding. Sarah had lunch with her father, Major Ronald Ferguson, who's off to Australia on Wednesday to visit her sister Jane. They lunched alone for ninety minutes. Both father and daughter displayed a commendable coolness under fire from a score of cameramen.

The Major is used to dealing with the press at polo events and Sarah seemed to be enjoying it all, which in the circumstances is a rather good thing. They didn't mind posing and Sarah had to remind her father she'd like to get into the car now please. Manoeuvring during this period of official 'no comment' isn't easy, but they achieved it with easy grace, Sarah rolling down the window for the photographers before driving off in the hope of losing them.

STAGE 3 Read the item in front of your class, who will comment on your performance.

STAGE 4 ## What is news? – a discussion

Work in groups of 4–6. Discuss these questions.

The News
Is this story 'news'?
How do you define 'news'?
Is it news if two people become engaged?
Is it news if someone is murdered? Or dies in a car crash?
Is the news generally full of serious and tragic stories?
Who decides what constitutes a news story?

The Royal Family
Why are people so interested in the Royal Family?
Should the Royal Family have more privacy from the news media? Or is it an important part of their function in today's Britain?

Reading the News

Here are four short items for you to practise *in pairs*. How can you tell that they are from local rather than a national news programme?

About Anglia,   March 17th 1986

Good evening. Norfolk sports car manufacturer group, Lotus, has announced major expansion plans. Over ten years they hope to double their work force and increase their output with the help of their new major shareholder, General Motors.

At the moment, Lotus produce 800 prestige cars a year, but today they unveiled ambitious plans to increase the annual output to around 7000. This will mean more jobs. The present work force of six hundred and forty will be doubled. Management have been promising expansion for some time. Now they have the financial backing of General Motors, their major shareholders, their plans are set to become a reality.

Train services between much of the Eastern Counties and London are experiencing delays following a train derailment in Essex. The accident happened near Goodways Station this morning, completely blocking the line. It was reopened just over an hour ago but delays are affecting services in and out of Liverpool Street from Norfolk, Suffolk and Essex.

Twenty civil servants at the passport office in Peterborough began a week-long strike today. They are protesting about the loss of a salary allowance which they say is worth £500 a year. The dispute will delay the issue of thousands of passports from the office which handles applications from East Anglia and parts of the Midlands.

A national strike by municipal bus crews has again been affecting services in the Eastern Counties. Bus drivers in Northampton, Colchester and Yarmouth are staging a second twenty-four hour strike, bringing services in all three towns to a halt. But in Ipswich bus crews have ignored the strike call and are working normally.

Your own news bulletin

Work in groups of 4.

STAGE 1 You are compiling news items for a local programme on events or incidents that have happened in your school. Choose about four items and write them down. Take an item each and practise reading it.

STAGE 2 When you are ready, each group reads its news items to the rest of the class. If you have a video camera, record your news programme.

STAGE 3 Discuss each group's reading. How like newsreaders did they sound?

The commentator's skill

A radio commentator has to give his audience a clear picture of what is happening. The most difficult of commentaries are those describing sporting events, where the action and drama suddenly explode; one second there may be nothing of significance happening, the next something important has happened.

The commentator therefore has to vary his or her tone, pace and volume, reflecting both the calm and the dramatic moments.

In pairs, practise reading these two extracts from BBC radio com-

mentaries to each other. In number 2, two people are speaking: **A** is
the commentator and **B** the summariser.

1 Lloyd again – right-hand court – she serves – wide to Martina's
backhand – too wide – at least a foot wide – Lloyd steadies herself –
serves again – it's good – comes back crosscourt – Lloyd backhand – deep to Navratilova's backhand – Martina lobs – too short –
Lloyd smashes crosscourt – and kills – a great shot – Martina
wrongfooted – first set to Lloyd – it took 23 minutes – I must say
she's playing with tremendous confidence and determination –
she – er – we could be in for an upset.

2 **A** Emburey again – well up – Richardson forward – driving – to
Gower in the covers – no power in the shot – Emburey seems
to be getting some turn – in he comes again – Richardson goes
back – dabs it to Lamb in the gully – he was looking for a
square-cut – it – it was too far up.

B Yes, he did him in the flight again. I just wonder if he ought to
try round the wicket – he – he could –

A Emburey again – Richardson forward – it pops – he's out –
he's – there was a tremendous shout – yes – he's out – caught

at forward short leg by Gatting – Richardson waited – all the
close fielders went up – they were confident he'd got a touch.

B I think it was pad, then bat – but Emburey's deserved that – no
question – he's bowled a good line – kept Richardson tied
down – he'd been fretting for the last few overs.

Your own commentary

STAGE 1 *In pairs*, practise your own commentary.
A performs a series of actions (simple movements, such as tying a tie
or shoelace, taking a book from a bag) while **B** describes what he/she
is doing. There is no need at this stage to vary the tone of voice, since
your partner is not doing anything dramatic.

STAGE 2 *Work in groups of four.*
Three people should work out a definite series of movements. They
might, for instance, mime a rescue of someone trapped in a vehicle.
The fourth person gives a commentary on the movements of the other
three. Here there will be a dramatic moment where the person is
finally freed and the commentary will change pace to reflect this.

STAGE 3 *Prepare a one-minute commentary*
The five pictures on page 70 show Miss Sellar (on the left) bathing
Coylum Marcus, the world champion Persian cat. Coylum is so strong
that Miss Sellar needs an assistant, Miss Pearson, to hold him in his
bath.

You are a reporter covering the world champion's preparations before
he defends his title.

Prepare a one-minute commentary on the bathing process. Coylum
will be making some loud noises as well as putting up a fight – he
hates his special blue rinse bath.

You may start before the first picture, if you wish, with the catching of
Coylum.

You may make your commentary funny, or you can describe it in the
type of voice used to commentate on royal occasions.

STAGE 4 *Tape your own commentary*
You could produce a tape of your own commentary on your favourite
sport. It must be on a real event; it is much easier to imagine rather
than describe. A commentary on a television coverage of sport with
the sound turned down would be a good opportunity to show your
skill.

4 Make a call

Speaking clearly and making yourself understood over the telephone
are very important: a job or a life might depend on a telephone call.

This section helps you in using the telephone and considers some
of the purposes of a telephone: buying and selling, making excuses,
making arrangements, giving good or bad news.

You will be asked to:

● consider the advantages and disadvantages of using the telephone
● give telephone instructions
● buy goods using the telephone
● take part in a role-play about making arrangements by telephone

Using the telephone

The most obvious point about telephoning, and one that is sometimes forgotten, is that the callers cannot see each other.

As a class, decide what advantages and what disadvantages this might have. Read out these telephone conversations and use them to help your discussion.

1   **A**   Hello. Yes?
    B   Is that Pete?
    A   Who's calling?
    B   Can I speak to Pete, please?
    A   There's no Pete here.
    B   Oh! What number is this?
    A   63825.
    B   Oh, sorry. 'Bye.

2   **A**   58324. Mrs Mayle speaking.
    B   Hello, Alison. I've just heard the bad news about Nick. How is he?
    A   They think he'll pull through now. But it was touch and go last night.
    B   What happened, Alison?
    A   Well, he was on his motorbike coming home from a night out when a car turned right in front of him, I think, without even indicating.
    B   I am awfully sorry, love. Is there anything I can do?
    A   No thanks, love. We're coping just about.
    B   Well, just remember, I can pop round any time you want anything.
    A   Thanks, Joan.
    B   Goodbye then.
    A   Goodbye. Thanks.

3   **A**   Mum, is that you?
    B   Katie, where are you phoning from?
    A   I'm in Madrid. We hitched down through France all right. But we had to get a train from Santander to here.
    B   Are you all right?
    A   Yes, fine, Mum. It's great. Trouble is I've run out of money.
    B   Oh! What are you going to do?
    A   Can you do me a favour? Can you get my bank to telex through £200 to a bank here in Madrid?
    B   Sure. Have you got that much money?
    A   Yes. The bank is . . .

4 **A** 4584. Phil Coulter speaking.

  B Hello Phil ... it's Dave. I hope I'm not disturbing you, but an urgent message came into the office after you left.

  A Is it so urgent I can't finish my bath and phone you back?

  B No, no, sure.

  A Give me fifteen minutes then. 'Bye.

  B 'Bye.

Discussion

What do you think the people in the pictures on the next page are talking about?

Telephoning instructions

STAGE 1 One member of the class sits at the front to make the first call. Everyone reads the situation below: *Feeding the dog*.

STAGE 2 Another person is chosen to answer the call. Give your name and number when you answer and, where relevant, the name of your office.

STAGE 3 Hold the telephone conversation. Do not look at each other. The rest of the class listens.

STAGE 4 The class discusses how clear and courteous the caller was and how polite and helpful the receiver was.

STAGE 5 Choosing two different people every time, try the other situations in the same way.

Feeding the dog

You have gone out for the day, leaving only a younger member of the family at home. You realise you have forgotten to leave any advice about feeding the dog. Ring home and give your instructions. The dog is fed once a day about four or five o'clock on a mixture of tinned dog meat and biscuits, half a tin of meat and a good handful of biscuits. The tins of dog food are on a bottom shelf in the pantry and a bag of biscuits is on the floor there. There is a tin-opener in one of the drawers of the kitchen sink unit.

Lost property

While travelling from Glendale on the number 17 Mirfield bus at ten

o'clock yesterday, you think you left an anorak behind. It has a logo – 'Stormgard' – on the top pocket and a hood lined with imitation blue fur. The anorak is light grey with blue striping. Ring the lost property office at the bus station and see if it has been handed in. If it has, arrange a time tomorrow when you can call and pick it up.

A holiday abroad

You want to book a holiday for four on the Greek island of Paros for a fortnight, June 20th to July 4th, and you have decided to stay at the Hotel Nikolas there. You would like two double rooms with two single beds in each. Ring the Glendale travel agency and ask if this can be done. Check with the agency that the deposit for the holiday is £26 per person to be paid at once, and that the balance of payment, £240 each person, is to be paid eight weeks before departure.

Making a complaint

You bought a scarlet sports shirt from a shop called 'Top Gear' about two weeks ago. The label inside gave instructions as to how the garment should be washed, recommending a 'hand hot' machine wash with a cold rinse. You followed the instructions carefully but put the garment into the washing machine along with other lighter-coloured clothing. The colour in the shirt you bought ran so badly that all these other clothes are now dyed pink. Ring 'Top Gear' to ask what they are going to do about it. (There will be opportunity here for the person taking the call to be helpful – apologising and offering to replace the shirt or return the money, and so on – or to deny responsibility. If 'Top Gear' will not help – which is, perhaps, unlikely – the person taking the call will have to have some convincing excuses for doing nothing.)

Hiring a group

As Entertainments Officer you are trying to arrange a concert to be held on the last Saturday in February. You have made enquiries and think you may be able to book a big name group. Now you have other spots on the programme to fill. A local group, 'The Satraps', is supposed to be good and you have heard that bookings are done by Nick Bell, the lead singer. You ring him to ask if the group is free to play on the night. You would like them to open the concert at 8 with a half-hour spot and then play again at round about 9.30 to 10 for another half hour. You could offer them around £50 for the performance. You cannot make a firm booking at the moment but after this enquiry you are making perhaps he can talk it over with the rest of the group and let you know later how they feel about it.

Buying by telephone

STAGE 1   One member of the class sits at the front, and chooses one of the articles to buy from the classified advertisements below.

STAGE 2   Another person volunteers to be the seller of the article. Give your name and number when you answer.

STAGE 3   Hold the telephone conversation. Do not look at each other. The buyer might wish to make an appointment to view the article, or might attempt to lower the price. The rest of the class listens.

STAGE 4   The class comments on the conversation.

STAGE 5   Repeat with different people buying different articles.

CARS FOR SALE

METRO L (W) 1981. Good condition. £1695. – Tel. 743 9080, after 6 pm.

1978 CORTINA GHIA automatic. 46,000 miles, MoT, radio, towbar, very clean inside and out. £850. – Tel. 1283.

1978 LANCIA BETA 4-door saloon. All round excellent condition. Long tax and MoT. Lancia alloy rims and wheels. Excellent engine. £400 or near offer. – Tel. Glossop 756043.

(R) MAZDA 929 4-door Saloon. Tax May 1986, MoT October 1986. £195 or near offer. – Tel. 933 1569.

1977 TOYOTA LIFT BACK Mechanically sound, MoT, November, 1986. £350. – Tel. Glossop 835286.

(N) CORTINA 1.6XL 12 months MoT, tax April, good runner, £225 or nearest offer. – Tel. 743 45702.

MOTORCYCLES

1984 SUZUKI 50cc 600 miles, taxed, helmet, back-box, front basket etc. £275, economical. – Tel. 933 67399.

CYCLES

GIRL'S 'HAWK' CYCLE. Suit from six years, excellent condition, £14.99. – 743 4965.

SPORTS EQUIPMENT/ CAMPING

SNOOKER TABLE 6ft. × 3ft. balls and cues, £50. – Tel. 023 565 9468.

DOMESTIC APPLIANCES

HOTPOINT Supermatic Twin Tub, auto rinse, as new, £75. – Tel. 743 1125 after 6pm.

TEFAL Mini Washing Machine, suit caravan or flat, fits on draining board, £14.99. – 176 Churchill St., Clayton.

TV, VIDEO Hi-Fi, washing machine and freezer sales and repairs – Tel. 877 7319 any time.

ARTICLES FOR SALE

PERSONAL STEREO Cassette Player. Good condition, cost £29, will take £10 or near offer. – Telephone 153 1266.

QUILT COVER, double size, blue with matching pillowcases, as new, £10. – Tel. 743 2786.

ROOF RACK AND BOX for car. Ideal for camping, never been used, genuine, £12.99. – 743 4059.

ROUND TEAK dining table and four chairs, very good condition, £70 or near offer. – Tel. 338 3541.

SANYO BETAMAX video with tapes. £100. – Tel. 338 1459.

SEVENTEEN SINGLE RECORDS mainly Shakin' Stevens, all ex-chart, good condition, £12.99. – Tel. 743 4085.

SHARPS STEREO PLAYER. Fit most cars, speakers inserts, £14.99. – 338 4107.

SHOWER BATH BASE POOL in blue, round type, £5. – 061-338 5271 after 6pm or weekend.

SMALL LILO DINGHY with paddles, footpump, unused. Ideal for holidays. Bargain, £14.99. – Please phone 301 11337.

TOWER AUTO SLO-COOKER. Only used twice, £14.99. – Phone 743 2284.

TREE LOGS for sale. – Tel. Glossop 35999.

TRICITY COOKER £40. Red carpet 80 per cent wool 4 × 5 £50. Bedroom suite, Maple wood £70. All in excellent condition. – Tel. New Mills 4389.

TWO DOUBLE GLAZED PANELS 5ft. 9in × 2ft. 2½in. leaf patterned. Unused £14.99. Pair or separate. – 061-338 1507 evenings.

BRAUN DELUXE FOOD PROCESSOR UK1. Hardly used £40 – cost £65. Tel. 469 5319 after 6pm and weekends.

Your own sale

Each member of the class writes a short 'For Sale' notice for the local newspaper, giving only a telephone number to contact. The advertisements are collected, re-distributed at random, and people ring their number to negotiate a sale or a meeting (which may be acted out later).

This role-play exercise is more difficult because

a   You will have no knowledge of when you will be called on to 'perform' until you hear your telephone number called.

b   You will probably not have any interest in or knowledge of the article you are trying to buy. You may have to make up a convincing story; for instance, why you need a second-hand pram.

The telephone – coping with a problem

STAGE 1   Choose three pairs from the class to take turns at being the bride's brothers or sisters.

STAGE 2   Read about the situation:

Three days before her wedding your sister, Diane, develops measles. The wedding, fixed for Saturday June 10th, will have to be postponed for a week. You will have to help with the necessary re-arrangements.

STAGE 3   Each pair chooses one of these arrangements to deal with:

1   Diane will not be strong enough to go on the walking tour in the Lake District that had been planned. Instead she and her fiancé, Maurice Cooper, will now spend three days in London – from Saturday 17th until Tuesday 20th. You have to:

   a   book them into a hotel;
   b   find a suitable train for them to catch after the reception, which is now planned for 11 a.m. on 17th June;
   c   arrange for a taxi to pick them up at the reception to catch the train;
   d   book two tickets for a show on Monday 19th (they like something light-hearted and preferably funny).

2   Your father has ordered three taxis – one to take the bride to

church at 9.45 and two to take guests from church to the reception at 10.45 a.m. These arrangements will now have to be postponed for a week. Unfortunately, your father has forgotten which taxi service he booked, although he knows it is one of the three listed below.

3   Most guests live locally, so they can be contacted easily. The five listed below, however, need to be contacted urgently so that they can cancel arrangements they have made and make the necessary new ones.

STAGE 4   The rest of the class chooses parts from the list below and answers calls about the wedding. Re-arrangements are unlikely to go entirely smoothly (an hotel may be fully booked; a relative very annoyed) but do not be too awkward.

Taxi services
Gopal Bros	Tel. 927032
Reliant	839211
Dexter Taxis	233097

(Your father has booked one of these for the wedding.)

Hotels
Grand Western	01 37926
Royal Beadle	01 93880
Central Park	01 33209
The Stag	01 29377

Theatres
Palace	01 23793
Marvel	01 27900
Merlin	01 32911

British Rail Enquiries   27950

Relatives

59732   Uncle Oliver – coming from Scotland. Has already booked an hotel in your town for the evening of Friday 9th June. Had arranged to go fishing on the following weekend.

22101   Auntie Marjorie – is bringing her husband and three children. Was to stay at your house on the Friday evening.

52988   Grandma – can be bad tempered; tends to think all illness is weakness – can be overcome by will-power. Was being fetched by your father.

64518   Grandad – rather deaf; does not like arrangements disturbed.

27909   Mrs Jackson – Diane's employer at the boutique in a neighbouring town.

STAGE 5 Each pair takes it in turn to make the calls. Callers do not look at each other.

Notes for the brothers/sisters

— Make sure you get the timings correct – particularly of the train and the taxis. Make sure that the hotel room is suitable and available for the three days. Find out what is showing at the theatres before making a decision.
— When you ring, simply ask for the number listed. The person chosen to act that part will then 'answer' his/her phone.
— Try to vary both tone and words. For instance, you will speak to grandad differently from the Grand Western Hotel.

The telephone – making an arrangement

STAGE 1 Choose two pairs from the class to take turns at making the arrangements.

STAGE 2 Everyone reads about the situation.

The manager of Glaxtons, a London factory making garden equipment, has left two of his staff to make arrangements for the visit of three directors of a German firm who are interested in placing a large order for Glaxton equipment.

The German directors (two women and one man) will spend two days in London. They will arrive at Gatwick Airport at 4 p.m. on Wednesday 9th April and their return flight is at 11 a.m. on Saturday 12th April. The manager wants them to be met at the airport, taken to a hotel and fetched to the Glaxton offices at 11 a.m. on 10th April, where they will spend the morning with him.

They wish to look round the factory, see a play in the West End and have a guided tour of London. They will eat at the hotel, except for lunch on the 10th and 11th, when they will be with the manager or looking round the factory. On those days they will have lunch in the factory canteen.

STAGE 3 Each pair plans what they have to do and divides the calls between them. (Each pair will take it in turn to role-play.)

STAGE 4 The rest of the class divide these roles among them and prepare to receive a query. For instance, the receptionists at the taxi services must know whether taxis are available at the times needed. The hotels must know availability and prices of their rooms. The theatres must know what is being performed, times, prices – they may be asked whether the play is suitable for foreign visitors.

Allan's Taxis	Gatwick Airport
Easy Rider Taxi Service	London Tourist Information
Trident Taxis	
Grand Hotel	Toxy Theatre
Balham Hotel	Sadlers Theatre
Gregory's Guest House	King's Theatre

Andrew Carson – Works Manager (will show the Germans round the factory)

Deidre Kenny – a personnel officer – speaks fluent German. She may be needed to interpret during the tour round the factory.

Alison King – in charge of the catering at Glaxtons.

STAGE 5   The first pair make their calls.

Remember these points:

— Mime holding the telephone and do not look at the person you are ringing.

— Do not make things too easy for the people making the arrangements, but do not be too difficult. Each hotel should, for instance, have some rooms free on the correct nights, but it's not unreasonable for there not to be quite enough. The secretary may even have to send the visitors to different hotels, or even have to make two of them share a double room.

Each pair should make an outline, with dates and times, of the plan for the visit when they have finished telephoning.

STAGE 6   The second pair make their calls.

STAGE 7   As a class, compare the two role-plays. Comment on how well the calls were handled and how clear, efficient and polite the callers were.

5 Have a good argument

Arguments can bring out the worst – as well as the best – in people. They reveal their prejudices or they simply insist on brow-beating others into believing what they believe.

This section looks at how to argue in an informed and unbiased way.

You will be asked to:

- consider the nature of argument
- challenge a one-sided viewpoint
- decide what are proper arguments
- use argument to solve problems
- use a formal structure to hold an argument
- take part in a role-play in which a jury argues about a case of car theft.

What is a good argument?

Read this scene.

A silly argument

A   Is this the place to come for an argument?
B   No.
A   Yes it is.
B   No it isn't.
A   Yes it is.
B   No it isn't.
A   Yes it is.
B   No it isn't.
A   Yes it is. It says so on the door.
B   No it doesn't.
A   Yes it does.
B   No it doesn't.
A   Yes it does. This is silly. I've come here for a *real* argument.
B   No you haven't.
A   Yes I have.
B   No you haven't.
A   Yes I have.
B   Time's up. That's £5 please.
A   That wasn't five minutes. You're supposed to argue with me for five minutes.
B   No I'm not.
A   Yes you are.
B   No I'm not. And I'm not arguing with you any more until you give me another £5.
A   Oh, all right. Here's £5. Now we can start a proper argument.
B   No we can't.
A   Yes we can.
B   No we can't.
A   Yes we CAN. Look, this is getting very silly. This isn't an argument. It's a series of flat contradictions, unsupported by evidence or reason. An argument is supposed to be an exchange of views on a subject of mutual interest to the participants, conducted with respect to the opposing party's point of view in a spirit of genuine enquiry,
B   No it's not.
A   Yes it is.

B   No it's not.

A   YES IT IS. This isn't an argument at all.

B   Yes it is.

A   No it's not.

B   Yes it is.

A   No it's not.

B   Time's up. Do you want another £5's worth?

A   No!

B   Yes you do.

A   No I DON'T. Goodbye!

based on a Monty Python sketch *The Silly Argument*

Discussion

Find as many reasons as you can why **A** is right in saying that he has not had a proper argument. How should you conduct an argument so that it is not a series of flat contradictions?

Your own silly argument

1   *In pairs*, choose a trivial topic to argue about; for instance, whether your shoes are light brown or beige in colour. Imitate the silly argument sketch.

2   Now choose a serious topic – whether smoking should be banned in all public places – and argue about it in the same way as the silly argument sketch.
   Is this how most people argue?

Warm up 1

Have an argument

*Work in pairs; label yourselves **A** and **B**.*

STAGE 1   **A** is selling potatoes by the roadside and doing a roaring trade. The potatoes are from the field behind. Set up your stall and decide how much you are selling your potatoes for and what your sales patter is.

STAGE 2   **B** actually owns the potato field. He/she arrives at the stall and questions **B** about what he/she is doing. Argue with words and not violence.

What do you think these two girls are arguing about?

Warm up 2

Give a reason

*Work in pairs; label yourselves **A** and **B**.*

STAGE 1 **A** describes his/her ideal house to **B**. It can be as unusual as you wish but it is set apart in huge grounds with a long drive.

STAGE 2 Set up a situation in which **A** is walking down the drive to find that **B** is a demolition contractor and is in the process of destroying your beautiful house.

STAGE 3 **A** asks **B** what he/she is doing. **B** must find a reason for demolishing the house. Have an argument with words not violence.

Challenging an argument

A biased person is someone who argues from only one point of view and refuses to admit any other.

Here is a biased argument about smoking:

> 'I don't think smoking's all that bad. I've never known anyone who's been harmed by it. I believe it keeps germs away, if you are in a room with someone with a cold, so it's good really. It can also calm you down in this hectic world and help you to relax from the stress of things like homework.'

Here is a challenge to it:

> 'Many people die of smoking-related diseases, even though you don't happen to know them. There is no evidence that smoking keeps germs away. In fact it is more likely to lower your resistance to some germs like bronchitis. How can smoking nicotine calm you down when it raises your heart rate?'

A one-sided argument

Work in pairs.

STAGE 1 **A** reads out one of these one-sided arguments below while **B** listens.

STAGE 2 **B** presents a challenge to the argument.

STAGE 3 **A** thinks up and presents a counter-argument.

STAGE 4 **B** challenges that argument.

STAGE 5 **A** and **B** now discuss their work. Could they have improved their arguments? Are they arguing a point of view they do not believe in? How easy is it to do this?

1 'The real place for women is in the home bringing up the children. It would help the unemployment situation, if jobs were offered to men first. I think half of today's vandalism is caused by women working and their kids running round in the street. Women have been made by nature to look after children and men haven't.'

2 'People are getting faddy about food: don't eat this and don't eat that. It drives you mad. I think you should just eat what you fancy. I mean, your body would tell you if it was bad for you; you'd be sick or something. "A little bit of what you fancy does you good," the saying goes. I think a lot of what you fancy does you more good.'

3 'Basically we need the Americans to protect us with their nuclear shield. We could never afford the arms to defeat the Russians, if they attacked us. Hitler attacked us because we were weak. Why

can't these CND supporters see this? Nuclear weapons have helped prevent war.'

4 'Nature conservationists try to stop the building of motorways and other things just to save a few animals and plants. Nothing would be built at all, if they had their way. You must have roads for all the cars and trucks, and you must have houses for people to live in. You can't stop progress. People come before nature.'

5 'If something is wrong and the police do nothing about it, I think you should take the law into your own hands. Take burglaries; the police do practically nothing where I live. What it needs is bands of citizens, vigilantes, in private armies making regular patrols. They could beat up any burglars they found. That would do more good than a small fine or a suspended prison sentence.'

6 'There are more murders today because they do not hang murderers. People wouldn't kill, if they knew they stood a good chance of being hung. It would cut down a lot of crime, like these bank robberies with sawn-off shotguns. If you kill a policeman or a child, you should automatically be hung to deter other people.'

When is an argument not an argument?

Perhaps the best challenge to an argument that someone has made is that it is not a proper argument.

Here is someone arguing that smoking does not damage your health.

'I don't think smoking is as bad as they say. I read in a newspaper that there's a doctor in America who says that it can actually do you good to keep smoking, because it calms your nerves. Anyway, my Uncle Tom smokes fifty a day and there's nothing wrong with him. I think if you enjoy smoking you should just carry on doing it.'

The speaker makes four statements but none of them is a proper argument against smoking.

Here is how he might be challenged:

1   'they say' is vague. Who is the speaker referring to?

2   'I read in a newspaper'   'a doctor in America'
Appeals to authority are very common in arguments, but who is to say whether this doctor is any more right than any other doctor? Or that the newspaper is not merely concerned to present a controversial viewpoint?

3   'my Uncle Tom'
You cannot argue from one particular instance. It is false to con-
clude that because Uncle Tom seems healthy now he will continue
to be so, or that his health means that everyone who smokes will
be healthy.

4   'if you enjoy smoking'
It may be reasonable to say continue smoking if you enjoy it, but
it is an irrelevant argument if what you are trying to prove is that
smoking does no harm.

Challenging arguments

Work in pairs.

STAGE 1   **A** reads out one of the arguments below while **B** listens carefully.

STAGE 2   **B** points out the false arguments.

STAGE 3   **A** continues by presenting proper arguments.

STAGE 4   **B** challenges any which he/she thinks are false.

1   'I think there are more jobs available now. The Government says
that the unemployment rate is falling. My brother got a job last
week, after being two years on the dole. They say there's more
jobs around. I think that everyone should work and not skive on
the dole.'

2   'You don't have to do a lot of exercise to keep fit; I saw it on the
television. I don't like a lot of exercise myself. I've always thought
it was bad for you. Look at that bloke in the paper who dropped
dead after going jogging.'

3   'Watching too much television is bad for you. It was in yesterday's
paper. Anyway, I know it's true, because my little brother has to
wear glasses and he used to watch television all the time. Anyway,
most of the programmes they show are rubbish.'

4   'People don't look after their pets properly. The RSPCA were
saying something about it. That woman over the road, she never
lets her dog out for a walk. I think people have pets for the wrong
reasons.'

Problem solving

Work in groups of 4–6.
Discuss these examples of local problems. You will need, first of all, to decide upon the background for your particular area and then to discuss possible solutions. There may not be a perfect solution: you may have to compromise.

Situation 1   Tidying up the environment

Background
What are the worst instances of vandalism, litter or unpleasant environments in your area? What are they caused by? Who is to blame?

Solution
What can be done to improve these instances? Who should do it? How much would it cost? Where is the money to come from?

Situation 2   Getting a job

Background
What is the state of employment in your area? Which group is particularly badly hit by unemployment? Who are the major employers?

Solution
What can be done to improve employment prospects in your area? Should employers be encouraged to move into the area? Should an odd-job scheme be set up to provide employment? What are the worst consequences of unemployment and what can be done about them?

Situation 3   Entertainment

Background
How do young people in your area entertain themselves? What facilities exist? How much are they used?

Solution
What facilities would you like to see for young people in your area? How should they be organised so that they are used properly? How should they be financed?

Situation 4   Communication

Background

Are there any local newspapers in your area? What information do they provide? Are there any other channels through which people can exchange local news and information? Do these channels work?

Solution

If you could set up a newspaper in your area, what would you like to see in it? Do you think a sense of community is important? How can you bring it about?

Drawing conclusions

When you have finished your discussion, prepare together one sentence which you think sums up the decisions you have reached. Each group reads out its sentence to the rest of the class.

Know your facts!

You cannot expect to be very successful in argument if you have not researched your case thoroughly. Many people give their opinion without much thought and then find themselves cornered in argument with someone who has thought and read a good deal more on the subject.

Topic of the week

STAGE 1 The whole class should decide upon a topic that is currently very much in the news.

STAGE 2 *In pairs*, follow your topic for a week in the newspapers and on television. Make a note of any points of interest or of fact. You will find it helpful to read as many different papers as you can, since each will present a different viewpoint – and quite likely – different facts. Watch current affairs programmes, such as 'Panorama', 'World in Action', 'TV Eye' and 'Question Time'.

STAGE 3 *In pairs*, sift through your notes and draw up a list of arguments for two or more possible points of view about the subject.

STAGE 4 *In groups of 6–8*, hold a discussion on your topic. Choose a chairperson who will keep order and give people the right to speak.

STAGE 5 When you have finished your discussion, discuss how you would summarise your argument in two sentences.

STAGE 6 Announce your two sentences to the rest of the class. This may provoke further discussion.

STAGE 7 In your groups, assess your discussion, bearing these points in mind:
— Did everyone speak?
— Did you listen to other people?
— Did you interrupt anyone?
— Did one person speak too much?
— How successful was the chairperson in keeping order?

Points of view

Prime Minister's Question Time – a class debate

The organisation

STAGE 1 *The class divides in half.* The two sides sit facing each other. One side is the 'Government' and the other the 'Opposition'.

STAGE 2 Choose one person from the 'Opposition' to be the 'Speaker'. He/she will now sit in the middle and chair the debate. The 'Speaker' is neutral and cannot give an opinion, but chooses people to speak and ask questions. It is important that he/she chooses people from both sides to speak, so that everyone has a fair hearing.

STAGE 3 Choose one person from the 'Government' to be the 'Prime Minister' and to reply to questions.

STAGE 4 Begin the debate. The 'Government' assists their side by making statements and questions in support of the 'Prime Minister'; for instance, 'I agree with the Prime Minister that ...'.

The 'Opposition' puts questions that try to find fault; for instance, 'What has the Prime Minister to say to the argument that ...?'

The topics

This arrangement can be used for debating any issue where there are two sides. Here are some examples:

1   The 'Government'
    — is defending newspapers' right to publish what they please
    — wishes to raise the cost of the TV licence
    — wishes to withdraw from the EEC
    — wishes to increase expenditure on schools
    — is lowering taxes.
    The 'Opposition' in each case is obviously not in favour of the 'Government's' motion. Use the structure to discuss other situations and issues.

2   The 'Opposition' are pupils. The 'Government' are teachers and the 'Prime Minister' is the Head.
    Suggested topics:
    — whether pupils should be allowed into school at lunchtimes
    — whether homework should be abolished
    — whether pupils should run their own school newspaper.

3   The 'Government' are Town Planners wishing to build a new road or a shopping precinct. The 'Prime Minister' is their leader. The 'Opposition' are local residents.

Assessment

When you have finished, consider either *as a whole class* or *in small groups* how successful your debate was. Did people listen? Were good points made or did the arguments deteriorate into abuse? Was each side able to represent its case?

A mock trial

The trial of John Major

Use the role-play to put what you have learned in this chapter into practice.

STAGE 1   Read the facts

On 16th April Andrew Piggott parked his Ford Capri in Barking. It was stolen. On the same night the car was found by Sergeant Pearson in a transport café car park near Romford. Inside the café was John Major, a man of 20, already known to the police.

After questioning, John was taken to Romford Police Station. While waiting to be charged, John was seen by Mrs Larkin who had come to make a statement about a break-in at her shop earlier in the evening. Mrs Larkin told the desk sergeant that John was one of the men she had seen at the break-in.

STAGE 2   Presenting the trial

Choose seven people.

Judge	Sergeant Pearson
John Major	Mrs Larkin
Defence Counsel	Joseph Barker
Prosecution Counsel	

The seven actors should give themselves time to prepare their parts, each deciding how he/she should say the lines. (The Counsels and the Judge may be played by boys or girls.) The rest of the class plays the jury.

Note
The script represents only extracts from the trial.

STAGE 3   Read the play

Clerk	Put up John Major. (*John is brought into the dock*) Is your name John Major?
John	Yes, sir.
Clerk	John Major, you are charged that on the sixteenth day of April 1986, you took a conveyance, namely a Ford Capri motor car, registration number ABE 139Y, the property of Andrew Piggott, for your own

	use, without the consent of the owner. Do you plead guilty or not guilty?
John	Not guilty.
Clerk	You are further charged that on the sixteenth day of April 1986, having entered, as a trespasser, a building, namely a shop at 19 Coston Avenue, Romford, you therein stole £25, the property of Mrs Larkin. Do you plead guilty or not guilty?
John	Not guilty.
Judge (*to John*)	You may sit down. Yes, Mr Gregg.
Prosecution	May it please you, Your Honour, members of the jury. I appear in this case for the prosecution and my learned friend, Mr Houseman, represents the defendant. I shall now call the evidence before you. Call Mrs Larkin.
Clerk	Mrs Larkin, will you take the Book in your right hand and read the words on the card.
Mrs L	I swear by Almighty God that the evidence I shall give shall be the truth, the whole truth and nothing but the truth.
Prosecution	Is your full name Edwina Larkin and do you live at 19 Coston Avenue?
Mrs L	That's right.
Prosecution	Did you leave your shop at that address locked up on 16th April?
Mrs L	Yes, and when I got back I found a pane of glass had been broken in the back door.
Prosecution	What happened next?
Mrs L	I opened the back door, went through and found a man trying to open the front door.
Prosecution	And the man turned round when he heard you?
Defence	Objection. Your Honour, my learned friend is leading the witness.
Prosecution	Very well. What happened when you saw the man?
Mrs L	He turned round and rushed past me. He pushed me out of the way. I came over all funny. I had to have a sit down.
Judge	We sympathise, madam. A very frightening experience.
Mrs L	It was, sir. I wake up at night thinking about it.
Prosecution	What happened next?
Mrs L	I went to the window and saw a car outside revving up. A man jumped in and slammed the door.
Prosecution	What sort of car was it?

Mrs L	Like my son's. It was a Ford Capri. They drove off in it. I found £25 missing and they'd left a glove.
Prosecution	Exhibit A, Your Honour.
	(*The Clerk shows Mrs Larkin a glove*)
Mrs L	That's the one.
Prosecution	And when you went to Romford Police Station did you see anyone?
Mrs L	Yes, I saw the burglar – him!
Prosecution	Let the records show that Mrs Larkin has pointed to the defendant.
Defence	Mrs Larkin, did you put the light on in the bedroom?
Mrs L	No, sir.
Defence	So the shop was in darkness?
Mrs L	There was a street light outside.
Defence	When you opened the door the man turned round?
Mrs L	Yes.
Defence	So the light would be behind him?
Mrs L	I could see him all right.
Defence	And he rushed past you immediately?
Mrs L	Yes.
Defence	So you only caught a glimpse of him?
Mrs L	Oh, no, there was no doubt about it – I was quite certain it was him.
Defence	In your written statement to the police, which I have here, you say, 'He looks like the man I saw in my shop.' You are now more certain than you were after the burglary?
Mrs L	I'm sure it's him.
Defence	Mrs Larkin, are you an expert on makes of Ford car?
Mrs L	I wouldn't say that.
Defence	Could you, for instance, know immediately the difference between a Ford Capri and, let us say, a Ford Cortina?
Mrs L	It was like my son's, a Ford Capri.
Defence	What are the distinguishing marks of a Ford Capri?
Mrs L	I knew it from its wheels, like my son's.
Defence	You are certain!
Mrs L	Yes, I am.

*   *   *

	(Sergeant Pearson is sworn in)
Prosecution	Sergeant, on April 16th this year, did you go to a café at the Romford roundabout?
Pearson	Yes, Your Honour.
Prosecution	What happened?
Pearson	Parked outside I saw a Ford Capri, registration number ABE 139Y. The car had been reported stolen earlier in the evening.
Prosecution	And inside the café you saw the defendant?
Pearson	Yes, Your Honour.
Prosecution	What did you do?
Pearson	*(refers to notebook)* I said to him, 'I would like to have a word with you about the Capri outside.' The defendant said, 'What Capri?' I said, 'The one that was nicked from a car park in Barking.' The defendant said, 'What's that to do with me?' I said, 'How did you get here?' He said, 'My mate Barker gave me a lift.' I said, 'Where is he now?' He said, 'I've no idea.' I said, 'Where do you live?' He said, 'Cubbage Street.' I said, 'How are you getting home? There's no bus service out here and you have eight miles to go.' He said, 'Perhaps you can drop me off if you're going that way.' I then cautioned the defendant and told him I was arresting him for the theft of the Capri. He replied, 'You prat. You've no chance of proving that.'
Prosecution	And what happened when you took the defendant to the police station?
Pearson	As a result of a conversation with Mrs Larkin, I charged him with the burglary. He said, 'That old woman must be a nut.' I asked him where he had been before visiting the café. He said, 'I'd been down the disco in Market Street.'
Prosecution	What did you say then?
Pearson	I said, 'But it was closed last week.' He said, 'Oh, I must have made a mistake.'
Prosecution	Did you show the defendant this glove?
	(Exhibit A is shown again)
Pearson	Yes, sir. He agreed to try it on. It fitted him.

*   *   *

Defence	Did you record everything that passed between you and the defendant in the café, Sergeant?
Pearson	I noted down a record of our conversation, yes.
Defence	How long afterwards?
Pearson	The same evening.
Defence	Perhaps you forgot to include that the defendant told you he had been in the White Swan at Romford with his friends on the evening of the theft.
Pearson	He did not say that.
Defence	Or you forgot to record it. When you asked the defendant to explain his movements that evening, he said he went to the disco in Market Street?
Pearson	As I've said, I told him that was rubbish.
Defence	Exactly – without giving him a chance to finish his explanation.
Pearson	He said, 'I must have made a mistake.'
Defence	I suggest that what he was going to say before you interrupted him was, 'I went down to the disco in Market Street and then found I'd made a mistake because it was shut. Then I went to the pub with my mates.'
Pearson	This is not true.
Defence	You mean you know he wasn't going to say that?
Pearson	I mean I didn't interrupt him as you suggest.
Defence	Thank you, Sergeant.

*   *   *

(*That is the end of the Prosecution's case. The Defence Counsel now calls John Major.*)

Defence	What time did you go out that evening?
John	I went to Romford about half past seven and met my mate Joe Barker. We decided to go to the disco but it was closed.
Defence	So where did you go?
John	The White Swan. Joe's girl was there, Andrea Machin.
Defence	When did you leave?
John	At eleven o'clock. Then we went to Joe's car. We were going to Southend to see Andrea's sister.
Defence	Did you stop on the way?
John	At the café I then decided I'd go home instead of going with them.
Defence	How would you get home?

John	Hitch a lift, but then Sergeant Pearson came and accused me of nicking the car. I started to tell him where I'd been, but he interrupted me as soon as I'd said, 'I went down the disco.'

*   *   *

Prosecution	When did you decide to go to Southend?
John	When we were in the pub.
Prosecution	Do you know Andrea well?
John	Not very well.
Prosecution	Is she coming here today to speak on your behalf?
John	She's gone away.
Prosecution	What time would you arrive in Southend?
John	I don't know.
Prosecution	You stopped at the café at half past twelve, so you would not have been able to arrive in Southend before half past one.
John	Yes, I suppose so.
Prosecution	Did Andrea's sister know you were coming?
John	No.
Prosecution	Did it occur to you that she might not be happy for you to arrive on her doorstep in the middle of the night?
John	I don't know.
Prosecution	Where were you going to stay the night in Southend?
John	At Andrea's sister's, I suppose.
Prosecution	So the three of you were going to visit someone you didn't know in the middle of the night and ask her to put you up?
John	Andrea knows her. It's her sister, isn't it?
Prosecution	Is she coming here today to give evidence that your friends visited her?
John	No; she couldn't come.

*   *   *

	(*Joseph Barker is called*)
Prosecution	You are Joseph Barker?
Barker	That's right.
Prosecution	Would you explain to the jury what happened on the night of the 16th April?
Barker	I went with John to the disco in Market Street but it was closed. So we had a few drinks.
Prosecution	Where?

Barker	In the White Swan. We met Andrea there and decided to visit her sister in Southend when the pub shut. We stopped at the café and John decided not to come. We went on without him. He said he'd get a lift back home. That's about it.
Prosecution	You remember clearly the events you've described?
Barker	Yeah.
Prosecution	What day of the week was it?
Barker	Wednesday.
Prosecution	Would it surprise you to know that the incidents we are concerned with took place on Saturday evening?
Barker	Oh yes, sorry. I remember now. It was the weekend.
Prosecution	When were you first asked to make a statement for Mr Major?
Barker	About a month ago.
Prosecution	And you'd say anything to help him?
Barker	No, just the truth.
Prosecution	You'd been in trouble with the police yourself, haven't you?
Barker	What do you mean?
Prosecution	Last year you were sent to a Detention Centre for stealing, weren't you?
Barker	That has nothing to do with this case.

*   *   *

(*That ends the defence case. The judge sums up the evidence for the jury.*)

Judge	Members of the jury, you have heard counsel for both sides. The two charges against the defendant should be dealt with as separate issues. On the first charge you have heard Mrs Larkin say she saw the defendant in her shop on the night of the burglary. Defence counsel has suggested she may have been mistaken, both in her identification of the defendant and the car she saw driving away. That is for you to decide, as is the evidence you have heard about the theft of the Capri car. On that charge, the defence case is simply that he did not take the car from the car park in Barking. He was never in Barking; he was in Romford or on the road to Southend. He explains his presence at the café eight miles from home after midnight, without transport, by saying he had been dropped off by his friend, whom you

have heard give evidence to that effect. If you feel Mr Major's account is true, then you will acquit him. If, however, you have no reasonable doubt that he was guilty of both or either of the offences, it is your duty to find him so. One last point. I ask you to retire and reach a verdict that is the verdict of you all. However, if that is not possible, I may accept a verdict of the majority. Now, members of the jury, consider your verdict.

STAGE 4   When you have read the play, divide into *groups of six*. Each six is a jury. The actors can be members of a jury as well. Each jury can either discuss the trial as themselves or take the roles below. Compare your verdict with the other juries.

1   young; thinks that the evidence of old people need not be taken seriously.
2   thought the defendant looked very smart and honest; feels you should only convict if there is sufficient evidence to make a hard and fast case.
3   has had brushes with the police, and is inclined to believe that they will twist their words if they need to.
4   is unable to ignore the fact that Joseph Barker was sent to a Detention Centre; thinks that thieves mix with thieves.
5   is annoyed that anyone should mistrust the evidence of a witness because she is old.
6   feels that the police should be supported by juries in their fight against crime and feels that anyone loitering outside a café late at night with no transport is rightly an object of suspicion for the police.

STAGE 5   Each jury discusses the case and reaches a verdict.

STAGE 6   Discussion

Discuss the following.

1   The reasons for the formal language and procedure in court. Think, for example, of the Defence Counsel's objection to the Prosecution Counsel's question to Mrs Larkin.
   'And the man turned round when he heard you?'
What did the Defence Counsel mean by 'leading the witness'? Why is it important not to lead?
(*In pairs*, practise questioning each other in the language of the court. Use a simple subject such as what you did yesterday –

remember that 'Did you go for dinner then?' is a leading question; 'Where did you go then?' is acceptable.)

2   How words, tone of voice and manner influenced your response. Did the judge and the lawyers manage to give an air of authority. Did John Major sound and look guilty? Did Mrs Larkin seem to be telling the truth?

3   Did the role-play jury take longer than the others to reach a verdict? Why might this happen?

4   What advantages and disadvantages do you think there are in the British legal system, now that you have taken part in this case?

Your own trial

STAGE 1   *In groups of about 6–8*, decide which one of you is going to be the defendant and what he/she is being charged with – for instance, theft, burglary, dangerous driving, smuggling, etc.

STAGE 2   Choose one person to be the Prosecuting Counsel and another the Defence Counsel. The rest of the group are witnesses, either for the Prosecution or the Defence.

STAGE 3   The group plans the case carefully. This will take some time. A trial is like a play; you have to plan your questions and answers beforehand, rehearse them and learn them.

1   Decide firstly whether the defendant is actually guilty or innocent and whether he/she will plead guilty or not guilty in court. (A defendant may plead guilty in order to get a lighter sentence.)

2   Reconstruct the events surrounding the crime. Decide who the witnesses are and what they saw.

3   Write up the defendant's account of what happened.

STAGE 4   Each group takes it in turn to present the case to the class, of whom one will be the judge and the rest the jury. The judge may ask his/her own questions and may advise the jury what to vote. At the end of each case, the jury is allowed up to five minutes to discuss the case before giving a verdict.

STAGE 5   After each case, the group presenting the case compares notes with the jury.

6 A matter of tact

This section looks at situations where to say the wrong word could result in embarrassment or misunderstanding or unhappiness.
   You will be asked to:

- try out a variety of situations which require tact

- evaluate your ability to handle a situation tactfully

- make an excuse gracefully

- break difficult news

Choose your words carefully

Situations

1 The homework

STAGE 1 Read this scene *as a class*.

Two girls sit chatting at break . . .

Alison Have you done your English homework?
Lisa What English homework?
Alison You know . . . that newspaper report we had to write.
Lisa Oh that! Oh, I forgot all about it!
Alison You're in trouble then. She'll go loopy, like she did last time.
Lisa I know. What am I going to say?

Here are two possible conversations Lisa might have had with her English teacher.

1

Miss Brown Right, hand your homework in to the front, please. Has ev . . . . . .
Lisa Miss Brown, I'm very sorry – I haven't done my homework. I'll have it done for tomorrow, though.
Miss Brown But it was supposed to be in today, Lisa.
Lisa I know, but it completely slipped my mind. I just didn't remember till break. I'm sorry, Miss.

2

Miss Brown Right, hand your homework in to the front, please. Has everyone done it? Yes? Good – that makes a change. (*pause*)
Lisa Er, Miss, no, I haven't.
Miss Brown Well, why not, Lisa?
Lisa I forgot.
Miss Brown You forgot? What do you mean you forgot?
Lisa I didn't remember till breaktime.

STAGE 2 *In pairs,* decide what you think the outcome of these two conversations would be. In which case might Miss Brown be more lenient? Give your reasons.

STAGE 3 *In pairs,* read out the two conversations and then continue each as you think appropriate. (You may change the names.)

2 The office thief

STAGE 1 Read this scene *as a class*.

An office. Mr Ackrill, the manager, is concerned about one of his employees, Mr Baker. There have been several thefts lately in the firm, and suspicion – but not proof – has fallen on Mr Baker: he has been seen near to the thefts in every case. Mr Ackrill decides to have him in his office to talk to him.

Mr Ackrill	Ah, Mr Baker. Do sit down . . .
Mr Baker	What was it you wanted to see me about?
Mr Ackrill	How are you getting on, Mr Baker? Job going all right?
Mr Baker	Yes, fine. I'm quite busy at the moment, in fact. Did you want to see me about anything in particular?
Mr Ackrill	Well, it's a bit delicate, actually. You know about this series of thefts we've been having . . . well it seems that . . . it seems . . . the finger seems to be pointed at you.
Mr Baker	What? Are you making an accusation, Mr Ackrill? I find this most offensive . . .
Mr Ackrill	Steady on . . . I didn't say you'd done it, it's just that one or two people have come to me and . . .
Mr Baker	You mean you've been listening to idle gossip? That's two offensive remarks you've made. If you intend to carry on in this way, I'll take my leave and consult my solicitor . . .

STAGE 2 *In pairs*, talk about this scene. How do you think Mr Ackrill handled the situation? What suggestions would you make to him about how to handle Mr Baker? Is there any evidence that Mr Baker is either guilty or innocent?

STAGE 3 **A** plays the part of the manager, and **B** plays the employee. Some of the employees will be 'guilty' of the thefts and some innocent.

STAGE 4 The **A**s discuss together these questions:
— Will you give a reason for calling your employee to the office? If so, what?
— Will you be direct or will you approach the matter indirectly?
— Will you try to find out whether your employee's home life is happy? If he/she is content with the job?
— What will you do if he/she becomes aggressive or suspicious? Remember, you do not know if the person is guilty or not.

You may all choose different ways of approaching the problem: this will add to the interest.

STAGE 5 **B**s decide together which of them will be guilty of the thefts and which innocent. It would be best if there were about half of each. (If you are innocent, do not try to play guilty in order to mislead your employer.)

STAGE 6   Play the scene.

STAGE 7   Each manager announces to the class whether his/her employee is guilty. The employees say whether the guess is correct.

STAGE 8   Discuss the success or failure of the various tactics used by the manager and how the employees responded to them. What advice would you now give to a manager in this situation?

Here are some more situations for you to try. They are all for pairs.

3   An unwanted present

STAGE 1   It is **A**'s birthday. **B** is a well-meaning relative who has bought a jumper as a present for **A**. **B** is sensitive and easily offended and is very keen that **A** should like and wear the jumper. **A** does not wish to upset **B** – but the jumper is awful!

STAGE 2   Play the scene.

STAGE 3   Discuss *as a class* how the **A**s reacted. Is there a correct way to behave in this situation?

STAGE 4   This time it is **B**'s birthday. **A** is a good friend of **B** and gives him/her a present. But **B** recognises that the present is the same one he/she gave **A** on his/her birthday.

STAGE 5   Play the scene.

STAGE 6   Discuss *as a class* how the scenes went. Did everybody react in the same way? In what circumstances does **B** tell **A** the truth?

4   A job well done

STAGE 1   **A** is the boss and **B** is the employee. **B** has come into **A**'s office full of triumph at a job well done. Decide between you what that job might be. It could be a new computer program for processing files in the office. Or it could be a set of accounts for last month's profits in a supermarket. **B** explains to **A** what he/she has done.

STAGE 2   **A** – turn to page 116 to read your instructions.

STAGE 3   Play the scene.

STAGE 4   Discuss *as a class* how tactful the **A**s were in handling the situation. What were the best lines of approach? How did the **B**s feel? How did they react?

STAGE 5   Try another scene and reverse the roles. This time **B** is the employer and has to tell **A** that he/she cannot have the promotion for which he/she is so eager.

5   A lovable pet

STAGE 1   **A** tells **B** about his/her favourite pet – its habits, what it looks like, its name, and what it eats. (Do not choose animals that are only confined to the house, such as goldfish.)

STAGE 2   **B** – turn to page 116 to read your instructions.

STAGE 3   **A** is at home. The doorbell rings. On the doorstep is **B**, the neighbour.

STAGE 4   Play the scene.

STAGE 5   *As a class*, discuss your scenes. Is it best to break bad news straight-away? Or to break it slowly? Decide what you would say if you were a police officer calling on someone to break the news of his/her close relative's death in a car crash. Or a doctor breaking the news to a patient that he/she is dying.

6   The job

STAGE 1   **A** and **B** are friends and have applied for the same job. Decide what job it is.

STAGE 2   You each receive a letter from the company: **A**'s letter congratulates him/her on obtaining the job; **B**'s letter offers regrets. **A** decides to visit **B** to see how he/she is taking the news. **B** hears the doorbell.

STAGE 3   **A** – decide whether you feel secretly triumphant over **B** – or openly triumphant. Are you sorry for **B**? Or do you think the best person won? **B** – decide how disappointed you are – very? or not much? Are you resentful of **A**? Or do you feel **A** deserved the job more than you?

STAGE 4   Play the scene.

STAGE 5   *As a class*, talk about the differences between the scenes. Did the scenes develop differently according to how disappointed **B** was, or how triumphant **A** was? Is a situation like this a test of friendship?

7   A language problem

STAGE 1   **A** is a foreigner. **B** is a member of the police, on the beat in Oxford Street, London. **A** asks **B** the way to Piccadilly Circus. **B** tells **A** to walk straight ahead as far as the large junction with Regent Street, to turn left down Regent Street. Right at the bottom of Regent Street is Piccadilly Circus. **B** realises, however, that **A** has not understood.

STAGE 2 Play the scene from the point where the foreigner asks the way to Piccadilly Circus.

STAGE 3 *As a class*, discuss the problems which the scenes revealed about communication between foreigners. What solution did the police find?

8   A family problem

STAGE 1 **A** is nineteen, has a job and lives at home. He/she has decided that it is time to move out and has found a flat and a friend to share it. **A** thinks the family home is too cramped for so many adults and feels he/she wants complete freedom.

STAGE 2 **B** is either the mother or the father. **B** senses that **A** is restless but fears that **A** is not yet independent enough to look after him/herself. Also **B** finds it hard to face up to the fact that **A** is no longer the child he/she has always cared for.

STAGE 3 **A** comes home after work one evening and breaks the news.

STAGE 4 Play the scene.

STAGE 5 *As a class*, talk about the scenes and how they compared. How did the parents respond to the news? What other situations do parents find difficult to deal with when their children reach their teens? Why do parents find these situations difficult?

Breaking bad news

How do you break bad news? Do you simply blurt it out? Do you lead up to it? Do you think of things to say which will make it seem less bad?

Read out these two conversations.

1
Visitor   How are you?
Patient   Not too bad.
Visitor   You'll feel worse in a minute.
Patient   Why?
Visitor   I've come to tell you your husband's had a bad smash up.

2
Visitor   Hello. How are you?
Patient   Not too bad. You look serious. What's wrong?
Visitor   I'm afraid I've got a bit of bad news.

Patient Oh no! Where's Marvin?

Visitor He couldn't come. He's had a slight accident.

Patient Marvin? Where? When?

Visitor Don't worry. He'll be all right.

Patient What happened? Tell me.

Visitor He's broken his arm and hurt his legs. He's got a few bruises.

Patient How did it happen? Where is he?

Visitor He's been in casualty but they've let him go home so it can't be all that bad. He was knocked down by a car.

Discussion

If you were a patient, which visitor would be more upsetting? Why? If you were the visitor, could you think of a kinder way of breaking the news? What might you say?

Situations

Work in pairs. Choose one of the following situations. Before you play the situation, discuss the best way to approach it.

1 Owning up

One is a pupil, the other is a headteacher. The pupil has started a fire in the school cloakroom accidentally. No one saw it happen but the pupil has heard that the Head is thinking of bringing in the police to investigate. He/she goes to own up.

2 Team captain

One is a captain, the other is a member of the team. The captain has to tell him/her that he/she is being dropped from the team for good.

3 Holiday

One is you, the other is your best friend. You have to break some holiday arrangements with your best friend because you have met a new boy/girl friend.

4 The job

One has a part-time job, the other is the employer. The part-time worker has to explain to his/her employer that he/she cannot come in next weekend. (Jobs are in short supply. Absence may mean the loss of this one.)

5   Police car

A parent has been into a police station to report the theft of his/her child's bicycle. Now he/she has to go back in to apologise for damaging a police car while driving off.

Relationships

STAGE 1   *In pairs,* read these two conversations between a salesperson and a customer in a shoe shop. Decide which you prefer and say why.

1
A   Good morning, (sir/madam). Can I help you?
B   I want a pair of black shoes.
A   Have you anything particularly in mind, (sir/madam)?
B   I saw a pair I liked in the window.
A   Right. If you wouldn't mind pointing them out to me.
B   There.
A   Ah, yes, part of our new range. What size, (sir/madam)?

2
C   Hello, Tosh. What do you want?
D   I'd be very grateful if you could show me some shoes.
C   Feel free. Have a look round, mate. We've got hundreds.
D   That's very kind of you. I did actually see a pair in the window that I liked.
C   You did, eh? Let's have a butcher's. Point 'em out, mush.
D   There. In that corner.
C   Right. How big are your feet, sunbeam?

STAGE 2   **Discussion**

Work in pairs. There are certain terms of address that we use in conversation to show how close or distant, friendly or unfriendly we feel towards the person we are talking to.

What do these terms of address show about the relationship to the person being spoken to? Is the person speaking friendly or more respectfully? How respectful? Is the person being spoken to older or younger or about the same age? Is the person someone in authority?

Mr Jones   Jones   Jonesy   Hey, you

Officer	Your Honour	love	Stiggy
sir	my dear	guv'	bighead
Mike	Michael	Good evening	Cheers

STAGE 3   *Work in pairs.*

In your discussion about the salespeople and the customers, you may have decided that the kind of language people use shows how they feel about their relationship to each other. Speaking to someone in authority, you show respect by using more formal language. Speaking to a friend, you probably use more slang.

The pictures on pages 110 and 111 show several different types of conversations taking place in a variety of situations. Choose two and first write the conversations you think the people are holding and then act them out. Remember that language, manner and tone will vary with the situation and the relationship between the two characters.

Suiting language to purpose

Read these two extracts from accounts of an accident.

1   I was proceeding down West Road towards High Road at 9.15 a.m. on the morning of Tuesday 6th March, when I saw a blue Vauxhall, registration CED 384Y, with its front wheel mounted on the pavement. The windscreen was broken and the front bumper was twisted. The owner of the vehicle, Mr John Brentford of 3 Acacia Avenue, Hawksley, was already standing on the pavement.

2   There's been a terrible accident in West Road. You could hear it miles away. I ran up and saw this bloke getting out of a car – he was shaking – and the car was up the pavement. The windscreen was all broken – there was glass everywhere.

Discussion

Work in groups of 4.

You will have no difficulty in identifying one as a police report given in court, and the other as a witness telling a friend. What clues in the use of their language allowed you to identify them correctly?

Using the right language – situations

Work in pairs.

1   An accident

STAGE 1   Invent the details of an accident – where it happened, who was hurt, how it happened, who witnessed it, etc.

STAGE 2   Take turns at holding these conversations:

A member of the police telling a relative about the accident.

A witness telling a friend.

A witness telling a member of the police.

A victim telling a friend/relative afterwards.

A member of the police being questioned in court.

STAGE 3   Perform one of the conversations in front of the class.
The class guess which situation is being performed and discuss the clues which helped them.

2   A boutique

STAGE 1   Invent details about the boutique – where it is, what it sells, who works there, its name, etc.

STAGE 2   Take turns at holding these conversations in the boutique:

The manager training a new assistant.

An assistant helping a polite, friendly customer.

An assistant dealing with an awkward customer who wishes to return goods.

The manager reprimanding an assistant for unpunctuality.

Two customers either chatting about how good the boutique is or complaining to each other that the service and goods are poor.

The manager giving the owner of the boutique a guided tour.

STAGE 3   Perform one of these conversations in front of the class.
The class guess which situation is being performed.

3   A hospital

STAGE 1   Invent details about a hospital ward – where it is, what it specialises in, what kind of people are in its beds.

STAGE 2   Take turns at holding these conversations in the ward:

A nurse waking a patient in the morning.

A senior nurse giving instructions to a junior nurse about what pills should be given to the patients.

A doctor talking to a patient about his/her progress. (Decide what is wrong with the patient before you start.)

Two doctors talking together about a patient's progress.

4   A bank

STAGE 1   Invent details about your bank – its name, situation, size, arrangement of space.

STAGE 2   Take turns at holding these conversations:

A customer withdrawing £50.

A customer asking the manager for a loan to buy a new car.

A customer asking the manager for a loan to start up a new business. (Decide what the business is before you begin.)

Speaking for different purposes

Can you identify?

Read the short pieces below and decide which type of speech each one belongs to. There is only one example of each.

a telephone call
a story
an instruction
a play
a street salesperson's patter
a political speech

a radio news bulletin
an interview
a television advertisement
a sports commentary
a television documentary

When you have identified them, discuss the clues of content and choice of words which helped you to your conclusion.

1   They used to tell the story about er a new manager who took over one of the pits and em – a – one man went in and he didn't know this was a manager and he – he let out and – swore at him and treated him as though he was just any old body and when he finished somebody says, 'Hey, that was the boss. I think you had bettah apologise. There'll be trouble.'

So at the end of the shift he went to see the boss and he says, 'Are ye the chap Ah tell'd to gan to hell?'

'Yes,' said the manager.

'Well,' he says, 'you needn't gan.'

2   'Come along, ladies! Why don't you come a little closer, dear? You won't see much there. Now then, now then! I've only got the best quality towels in the country. You don't believe me? Have a feel then! Come along! Don't be shy! I've got the full range of colours: something to suit every bathroom. You want a green one, do you? Hang on, missus! I haven't told you the price yet. If you went into any big department store this bath towel would cost you £14; wouldn't it? You know it would, ladies. Would I sell it to you for that? No, ladies! I wouldn't make a living if I sold them to you for that price, now would I? I'm not even going to sell them to you for £10. Oh, you'd buy it for £10, would you? Hang on, missus! You've got money to throw away, haven't you? No! For you ladies, these towels are going for £8 only.'

3   'Look, first of all you need to decide what temperature you want your wash at. You're doing just socks and shirts, are you? Well,

you just want to turn that knob to the two dots. Right? Oh! Now put the clothes in the machine and close the door. Right then. Erm, next we put the powder in. You want a cupful in that hole and another one in that one. Now put a capful of fabric conditioner in that other hole. Right. Press that switch there and we're off! It'll be ready in about half an hour.'

4 **Father** Hello, stranger.
Terry Hello, Dad.
(Father holds door open for Terry to walk into living room)
Father This is a surprise. I didn't know you were coming today. Your mother didn't tell me.
Terry She didn't know.
Father This is a surprise.
(Father shuts the front door and then pushes it to make sure it has shut securely)
Terry Where is she?
Father In the kitchen. *(Father turns to face Terry)* I'm glad you've come. Now I can get out of the drying-up.
Terry You won't get away with that.

John Hopkin from *Talking to a Stranger*

5 **Jeff** 63230. Jeff Lord speaking.
Bill Hello, Jeff. Look, I'm sorry we're not going to be able to make that drink tonight. Our babysitter's let us down.
Jeff Oh, that's a shame. Not to worry, though. Can we arrange another date?
Bill Yes, fine. What do you suggest?

6 Reports are coming in of a car bomb explosion in Lebanon. It went off in the port of Jounié near Beirut in an area busy with lunchtime crowds. Details are still confused but it is believed that at least nine people have been killed and scores injured.

7 **A** Have you had a Saturday job before?
B No, not a Saturday job. I used to do a paper round in the mornings.
A So, do you know what the job would involve if we gave it to you?
B Well, no, not really. Only what it said in the advert.
A Well, you would start at nine. We do, of course, expect staff to be punctual. Persistent lateness may well mean a fine. After clocking in, you would make your way to the stores at the back of the supermarket . . .

8 Don't risk trouble and strife! A trunk call from *The Elephant* will remind you of that important birthday/anniversary a week in advance. Ring him at 01 237 9002.

9 'It's two and a measure ... Burton only needs two for the set ... I don't think Harby can hope to draw past his own bowl ... he's going to fire ... all or nothing ... here it comes ... he's on line... he's got it, I think ... yes ... Burton's bowls scattered left and right ... and the jack ... a dead end ...'

10 The main purpose of the common agricultural policy was to ensure the availability of food supplies by increasing agricultural productivity.

   This was just one of the advantages that the government of Edward Heath sought when the United Kingdom joined the Common Market in 1973. This step was to transform British farming, British food supplies and ultimately the prospects for British health.

11 'Mr Speaker, I share my Honourable friend's views. But in view of recent events, has not the time come when we should reconsider our policy? Where is the sense, the fairness, the justice in continuing to cut jobs in this industry? Would it not be a regrettable move to ignore what is happening in that part of the country? I call on my Honourable friends to put past divisions behind them and to rethink our strategy on this issue.'

---

*Instructions for **A** in Situation 4 on page 104*

A sees that, in fact, the job has been carried out badly and has to tell **B** as tactfully as possible.

---

*Instructions for **B** in situation 5 on page 105*

You are **A**'s neighbour. You must tell **A** that his/her pet is dead. Decide upon the circumstances in which you find the dead pet.

7 Working together – two role-plays

In this section you will be practising many of the skills you have learnt in this book.

You will be asked to:

- cooperate as a group
- handle situations tactfully
- argue your point of view
- report back
- solve problems
- make decisions
- ask questions
- follow an argument
- adopt different registers
- lead a group
- read a play
- evaluate your work

The advertising agency

These short scenes are intended to help you understand the jobs of people who are responsible for poster, TV and radio advertisements. Either read them or act them out. As you are doing so, decide which role you would like to play in the group simulation work which follows.

Scene 1
Miss Walsh is from TopSport Limited. She is meeting Mrs Jakes of the Mayfair Advertising Agency. TopSport's manager has previously telephoned the agency saying that a company representative would call to discuss the promotion of their new unbreakable tennis racquet.

Read this extract from their conversation.

Mrs J   How unbreakable is 'unbreakable'?

Miss W   Well of course it can be broken if you set out to break it. But we've developed a toughened nylon that will survive years of battering from the fastest tennis balls at whatever tension the strings are set.

Mrs J   Has that increased cost?

Miss W   By about 10%, but of course it depends how well the product sells. If we could sell directly from the factory we could even undercut the traditional racquets.

Mrs J   The trouble is that a well-directed media campaign could start a response; but you may need the retail outlets to keep the product in the public view.

Miss W   What do you suggest?

Mrs J   I'd assume the time for a media campaign is spring – we'd be able to confirm from market research that most racquets are bought then. You say you are prepared to spend £300,000 on advertising. That would mean television is out, unless we spend a limited amount on the London region; it may be, for instance, that tennis is most popular in the Home Counties. It might be worth it then. Local radio is often effective at drive time, and is certainly cheaper.

Miss W   What's 'drive time'?

Mrs J   Early morning and late afternoon, when people are driving to and from work.

Miss W   You see, we think our best customer is likely to be the child or teenager, maybe the first-time buyer, who can't afford for the racquet to break, so I'm not sure about radio.

Mrs J   You're probably right, but perhaps the parents do the actual buying. We'll do some research and a costed recommendation. It may be that a combination of various types might be best.

Miss W Well, we'll hear from you then. I'll leave you these sample ranges. There's a range of three, the cheapest at £40 and the dearest at £80; that's as low as we can go.

Scene 2

Two weeks later, Mayfair Advertising Agency has produced a report recommending a campaign during May of:

a 30-second advert on Thames TV;

a 1-minute advert on radio in the London and central and northern areas;

a poster campaign throughout the London area.

Their research has shown that tennis is more popular in the south and that teenagers are taking up the game more competitively.

Jane Jakes leads a team of four discussing the advertisement: Sue, Peter, George and Jane herself.

Jane I don't really like 'The Unbreakable'; we need something that gives the idea of toughness and power without inviting people to try to break it.

Peter The Rambo.

George Rambo's hardly right for tennis.

Peter But aren't we trying to get away from the patball image of tennis?

Sue Why not call it 'The Power Driver'?

Jane What about the reliability aspect? We'll leave the name for the time being. I'd like to discuss the adverts.

Sue Are we using a tennis player for the TV?

Jane I don't think so; the budget wouldn't stand it.

George And most top players bash their racquets on the ground. We don't want the unbreakable breaking.

Peter I think we ought to try the tragic consequences angle. You know, Virginia's in the final of the Okehampton Ladies' singles and her racquet smashes – has to scratch.

Jane Surely somebody would lend her one.

Peter Yes, but you can't play with a borrowed racquet. It wouldn't feel right.

George Maybe we should stress the personalised racquet angle: 'The Durable' – or whatever we're calling it – 'racquet for life'.

Sue Sort of 'Make a friend of your racquet'. What about a mixed doubles situation? Jim's asking Wendy to be in the mixed doubles with him. She's all excited, her racquet busts, Harriet becomes Jim's partner and then wedding bells and Wendy ruined for life because she didn't pay that little bit more.

Jane   We could try a mock-up of something like that; we mustn't overdo the 'ruined for life' aspect. What about radio?

George   I thought of a series of noises. Lots of famous players grunt when they hit the ball.

Peter   Grunt!

George   Yeah, they go 'Ugh, ugh!', So we could have 'Ugh, boink, ugh, boink, ugh, boink, ugh, crash, eearch!'

Peter   'Crash' being the splintering racquet and 'eearch!' the player's reaction?

George   Yes. Then a commentator with a soft voice ...

Sue   Saying, 'He's broken another racquet. He's gone to the umpire's chair. I think he is ... he is going for a "Durable".'

George   Then a voice-over saying, 'Another convert. He's chosen a friend for life' – something like that.

Jane   Then a few more 'ugh, boink' noises, applause and voice-over 'Game, set and match to Durable'. Not bad. You work on that, Peter. Now, what about the posters?

Peter   I think we ought to concentrate on the three qualities available.

George   That worries me. If none of them breaks, what's better about the expensive one?

Jane   It's graphite; the cheapest one has a wooden frame.

George   Won't it break?

Jane   I think we have to remember that the string is the unbreakable part. The frames will smash as easily as any others.

Sue   Shouldn't we do something about the different colours of the handles. There's the red, blue and green. Shouldn't we say, 'Available in three finishes: petal red, savoyard blue or sea green'?

Jane   The red one's the cheapest; I don't know if they can do all three colours for each racquet.

Peter   Are we calling the cheap one 'economy' and the dear one 'deluxe'?

Jane   Maybe. But we want to stress reliability above all. We don't want to distract customers from that.

Scene 3

Three weeks later, Topsport have approved Peter's script for the 30-second television advertisement. Jeremy is directing the film. He has a camerawoman, Angela, and his two main actors, Sally and Gerald. Peter is advising. They have hired a tennis court at Eastbourne.

Peter   The trouble is, Sally might look twenty thousand pounds – or whatever they're paying – in a tennis dress, but she can't hit the blasted ball.

Jeremy	You're right, I know. Angela, just get the best shot you can of her running for the ball. Then we'll take close-ups of the ball pinging off the racquet. Peter, you can hit the ball for us.
Angela	I'll have to keep his hairy arm out of shot. And he'll have to put green nail varnish on – or she'll have to take hers off.
Jeremy	Don't make difficulties. Let's do the tearful bit. Sally, get hold of this broken racquet.
Sally	What do I do with it?
Jeremy	Just look at it, burst into tears and wimp off to the bushes. Gerald, are you ready?
Gerald	All set and game.
Jeremy	Don't be clever. Have you got the racquet?
Gerald	You mean the Sure Thing?

Jeremy	The Sure String – not Thing – you fool! Ready, Angela? Right. Take seventeen. Off you go, Sally.
Sally	Oh, my racquet!
	(*She runs tearfully to the bushes. Gerald steps out from behind the bushes*)
Gerald	You mustn't be such a bad loser, my dear.
Sally	I didn't lose. It's my racquet.
Gerald	The strings gone again? Ever tried Sure String?
Sally	No. Aren't they terribly expensive?
Gerald	It's worth paying a little more to make a friend for life. Try this.
Sally	Oh, thank you.
Gerald	Now go back and win. One thing's sure, you'll never break a string.
Sally	And I might have made two friends for life.
Jeremy	Cut. Sally, look at him a bit more meaningfully when you say 'two friends'.
Sally	I might be able to if he stopped waving that bat thing in my face.

Making advertisements

Work in groups of 4. Each group will simulate the process of making advertisements from customer approach to finished product.

STAGE 1 Choose a product for each group. Something with interest for young people would be best – a magazine, a shampoo, a drink, for example.

STAGE 2 Choose two people to represent the product's company. They talk to the rest of the group (who are the advertising team) about the features of the product and the amount they can afford to spend. When this discussion is finished, these two then become part of the advertising team.

STAGE 3 One person should be chosen to lead the advertising team's discussion on the best way to sell the product. Discuss the name, the type of people who will buy the product, and how best to reach them through the various media.

STAGE 4 At the end of the discussion, divide these jobs among you:

a write a report on the cost of advertising in various ways, including some figures about the sex, age group most likely to buy;

b write a radio script for the product;

c write a TV script;

d design a poster.

Set the scripts out like this:

Radio script
A   Meeow! Meeow!
B   Let the cat in, Fred.
A   I've only just let it out.
B   Well, it wants to come in and I'm in the bath.
A   And I'm watching the football.
        (*scratching noises*)
A   It's scratching your new paint, dear.
B   Oh, all right, I'll go.
A   Couldn't you fit a cat door, Fred?
B   How could I fit a cat door?

C   Even a Fred could fit a cat door with the new *1001 Jobs Made Easy* book.

        (*purring noises*)
A   It's all right, it's come in by itself.
B   How could it do that?

C   In fact, a cat of average intelligence could fit its own cat door using *1001 Jobs Made Easy*, only £3.99 from all good newsagents.

A 60-second radio advertisement would need approximately two pages of script. For television scripts, split your page into VISION and SOUND. Describe the camera shots under VISION (e.g. girl looks at broken racquet, bursts into tears) and try to synchronise the sound with the vision.

STAGE 1   As a group, examine and discuss the scripts and poster. Two of the group could become the product's company representatives again and comment on what they have seen and heard.

STAGE 2   Act out one or more of the adverts. Tape the radio advert, if possible.

STAGE 3   Each group should show, or play, its most successful advertisement to the rest of the class for comment.

The small company

Running a business

'Festivities' is a small company which makes Christmas decorations. The director has decided to diversify because the company is in some financial trouble. He/she has appointed a team of people to be responsible for designing and making a new and expensive cracker which will sell at £25. There are three teams responsible for the design and creation of the cracker.

Team 1 is responsible for the wrapping which will cost a maximum of £5 per cracker.
Team 2 is responsible for the trinket which will cost a maximum of £10 per cracker.
Team 3 is responsible for the joke or proverb.

There is also a sales team (4) responsible for marketing the product.

In charge of each team is a supervisor. In overall charge of the teams is a manager and an under-manager. Each of these has a secretary.

STAGE 1   Divide these roles among your class:
Director
Manager
Under-manager
Four team supervisors
Members of the four teams
Director's secretary
Under-manager's secretary

STAGE 2   You have a job. Now give yourself a character. Choose from the characters below. When you have chosen, read the characters chosen by other members of your team. Make sure that you have a good mix in your team. (Discuss which are not suitable for some of the roles.)

1   Not prepared to accept new ideas, this person is unhappy at having to leave the work at which he/she was happy for this new project. Will need careful managing.
2   Appears to be a good listener, but in the end always makes his/her decision regardless of advice. A little stubborn. Perhaps worried that people do not respect him/her.
3   Keen, competitive, ambitious, aiming for the top. Always earns the highest bonus for hard work and exciting ideas.
4   Always late; lazy. Constantly excusing him/herself. Daydreams during work.

5   New to the company; quiet; a little shy; not quite sure what is expected of him/her. It will be interesting to see how this person develops as he/she gains confidence.

6   Cheerful, enthusiastic, kind. Goes out of his/her way to be helpful to others. Union representative.

7   There are suspicions that this person is not totally honest. Good at getting others to do his/her work.

8   Very persuasive and full of energy. Pushes other people to work to their limit. Full of charm.

9   Good at handling people. Tactful, polite, considerate. Likes people and is prepared to negotiate with them.

10 Negative; a moaner; always expects the worst to happen. Worked with the company a long time.

STAGE 3   In order to acquaint yourself with your role, write down the answers to these questions:
How old are you?
How long have you worked for the company?
Do you enjoy your job?
What is your attitude to this new project?

STAGE 4   Set up your 'offices'. Decide how you will arrange your desks and chairs. Who has the biggest office? Do the supervisors want to show their authority by sitting apart from the other members of the team?

STAGE 5   Read all these job instructions, but particularly the one which applies to you.

Teams
1   Wrapping – what colour? What material? Size? Shape? Budget: £5 each.
2   Trinkets – what trinkets? Watches? Jewellery? A variety? Research what the public wants in crackers. Do you make the trinkets or buy them? Budget: £10 each.
3   Jokes – what kind of jokes? What audience are you expecting? Would personalised messages be successful?
4   Sales. Who are you selling to? How will you advertise? Newspapers? (which ones?) TV? What angle will you take? What are your sales targets? How many must you sell?

Supervisors
Lead the discussion and keep your team working.

Manager and under-manager
You are preparing for the annual salary review, in which the best workers (no more than 20%) will receive an extra bonus, whereas the

laziest workers will receive no extra increase next year. You will need to decide whom to reward. Your job is also to ensure that things are running smoothly, to deal with complaints within the teams, and receive regular reports of progress.

Secretaries
You take messages, fetch people, and make notes of important decisions.

Director
Keep the pressure on the managers – this project is vital to the success of the company. Check on their progress and that everyone is working to capacity. You have the power to dismiss an employee, but you must first consult the union representative.

What happens in the role-play

STAGE 6 Start your role-play discussion. Remember that you can visit other teams if you have a query. (You cannot see the director, however, without the permission of the manager.)

STAGE 7 When you feel that you have discussed everything necessary, hold a meeting of the whole project in which the supervisors report to the managers and director the decisions their teams have made.

STAGE 8 Out of role, hold a discussion about
— what you found interesting;
— whether you thought a company would be run like this;
— whether you found it difficult or easy to play your character;
— whether people worked together or were uncooperative;
— who you thought had the hardest and easiest jobs.

8 Finding out the truth

Asking questions

STAGE 1 Here are some different ways of questioning people. *In pairs*, read the scenes. What do the questioners wish to find out in each case? What are the differences between the types of question? What situations is each appropriate for?

A

Lost property lady	What colour is your purse?
Mrs Parker	It's black.
Lost property lady	What's it made of?
Mrs Parker	Leather – it's good quality leather.
Lost property lady	How big is it?
Mrs Parker	About as big as that purse there.
Lost property lady	And where did you lose it?

B

Head	What do you think we should do about this boy?
Teacher	Well . . . I think a letter home to the parents would be a start.
Head	Is it possible he didn't take the purse?
Teacher	It's possible . . . we can't prove it.
Head	So what do we say to the parents?
Teacher	That's the difficulty. I think we should simply tell them everything we know.
Head	How do you think the parents will react?

C

Social worker	It's a lovely place they've given you – really cosy – you must like it here?
Old lady	It's all right but it's lonely. You never see anyone.
Social worker	I know what you mean. You have to make more of an effort when you get older, don't you? But don't you think you should make an effort?

Old lady	I don't know what you mean – effort! I can hardly walk. I can't go gadding about in the streets.
Social worker	No, but you might be a bit more friendly to the Meals on Wheels when she calls, mightn't you? Why don't you want to talk to her?

A role-play

Keep in mind the play and the work you have done on questions during this work.

The situation

STAGE 1 Early one morning, two women in the same town go to their babies' cots and find their babies dead. There is no connection between the deaths: it is pure coincidence. The mothers phone their doctors who examine the babies and find the cause of death to be suffocation: there are no obvious signs of ill-treatment. The doctors call an ambulance and the babies are taken away. Then the police and social services are informed. It does not take long for the local newspaper to hear of the deaths. Soon, the parents are having to deal with a succession of people – police, social workers, journalists, neighbours. What the police want to find out, with the help of social workers, is whether the babies died naturally – cot death – or whether their parents killed them.

In one case, the death is natural and in the other it is not, but only the parents know the truth.

STAGE 2 The class divides into two groups. Each group will take part in the role-play, simultaneously.

STAGE 3 Allot the following parts among the group:

the parents of the two babies (4 parts)
police (2–4 parts)
social workers (2–3 parts)
journalists (2–3 parts)
neighbours (3–4 parts)

STAGE 4 Read the instructions and roles for your parts. Set up your classroom as best you can to suggest the houses and offices of the various groups.

The characters

The parents

Instructions
1   Each couple choose one of the roles below.
2   Decide which couple killed their child.
3   Choose your names.
4   Answer the questions below.
5   Set up your house.

Roles
Couple 1 — quiet, polite, good neighbours, look after house carefully; father works (where?) – he seems a little nervous – smokes; comfortably off, perhaps some strain between couple (why?); both had been keen to have a child.

Couple 2 — noisy, outgoing, lots of friends, untidy, play loud music (neighbours complain of noise); father out of work but mother has a job (what?); both like going to the pub for a drink; generally considered easy-going but good-natured.

Questions
What was your baby called? Who looked after it? If you killed it, why? What were the circumstances of its death? What kind of baby was it? crying? placid? What will you say to the police? the neighbours? the social workers?

The police

Instructions
1   Choose your role from below.
2   Set up your office.
3   Decide what questions you will ask the parents.

Roles
Police 1 — young, new to the force, follows lead of senior officer, sympathetic.

Police 2 — senior officer, experienced at handling sensitive situations, realises nothing to be gained from antagonising parents.

Police 3 — solid, reliable, not a great deal of imagination, full of feeling but no tact.

Police 4 — tactful, good at gaining people's confidence.

The social workers

Instructions
1   Choose your role from those below.
2   Set up your office.
3   Decide on your line of approach with the parents.

Roles
You are concerned for the truth but also worried about blame attaching to the social services. Neither family has come to your attention before.

Social worker 1 — overworked, underpaid, tired, heavy case-load, well-meaning but a little impatient.

Social worker 2 — brisk, energetic, no-nonsense type, but sympathetic underneath.

District nurse — has visited both families since the births, recorded steady weight gain, satisfied that bonding between mother and baby seemed fine; saw no cause for alarm; a hard-working, caring person.

The neighbours

Instructions
1   Choose your role from those below.
2   Decide what your attitude is to what happened next door.
3   Set up your house.

Roles
Neighbour 1 — considerate, discreet, not willing to gossip but will help out in need.

Neighbour 2 — always ready to spy and gossip, always quarrelling about household jobs, ready to think the worst of other people.

Neighbour 3 — talkative but very good-natured, does not mean any harm.

Neighbour 4 — does not like visitors, solitary, quiet.

The journalists

Instructions
1   Choose your role from those opposite.
2   Choose the name of your paper.
3   Set up your office.
4   Decide on your line of approach with the parents.

Roles
You are not interested in the *truth* but in what will make the most exciting story.

Journalist 1 — experienced and hardened, persistent, not moved by tears, keeps pressing for answers.

Journalist 2 — young, new to paper, so far only written about coffee mornings and weddings, put off by senior colleague's manner.

Journalist 3 — knows that charm is needed in these sensitive circumstances, good at getting people to talk about themselves.

The role-play

STAGE 5   The authorities will have to divide up to visit both couples. Remember that although you will have to ask factual questions, it is the more open questions that will enable you to find out the truth.

The journalists must not obstruct the police's work: they may have to speak to a neighbour first.

Everyone's task is to find out what has actually happened.

STAGE 6   Start your role-play at the moment when the police go round to visit the parents.

STAGE 7   When the questioning is complete the police and social workers return to their offices to discuss what they have discovered and prepare a report.

The journalists return to their office to decide upon a headline and on the contents of their article.

The parents and neighbours talk together about their treatment by their visitors. Were they treated with sympathy and tact? Was the treatment as you expected?

STAGE 8   As a class, hold a discussion about what you have been doing.

Each group of police, social workers and journalists reports on what they have discovered about the couples. The parents and neighbours comment on the treatment they have received. At the end of discussion, the parents can tell the group which couple killed their baby and why.

Index

Accent   45
Advertisements   118–23
Arguments   81–100
   challenging   84, 87
   facts   89
   one-sided (bias)   85–6
   PM's Question Time   90
   problem-solving   88–9
Assessment   1–9
   pupil's self-assess-
     ment   8–9
Body language   41
Breaking bad
   news   106–7
Clear speaking   56
Committee minutes   62–3
Consonants   56
Consumer survey   30–1
Dialect   45, 59
Debate   90
Demonstration   49
Feelings   53
Group discussion   3, 9
     (and in most sections)
Instructions   49, 73
Interviewing   14–33
   jobs   21–33
   press and TV   15–20
Language, suiting to
   purpose   109
Oral record chart   6–7
Persuasion   36–7

Persuasion   36–7
People, judging
   relationships   108–9
Poetry speaking   56–8, 60–1
Questioning   127–1
Reading to an
   audience   51–67
   commentating   67–9
   news   63–7
Role-play   3, 9,
     77–9,
     92–100,
     118–22,
     128–31
Speaking to an
   audience   2, 8
   different purposes   113–16
Story telling   43–7
Tact   101–8
   breaking bad news   106–7
Talks   35–43
   current affairs   40
   hobbies and
     interests   37
   planning   40
   preparing   38
Telephone   72–80
   arrangements   79–80
   buying   76–7
   instructions   73–5
   problem calls   77–9
Tone   52, 57